BONAVENTURE
The Life of St. Francis

Foreword by Donna Tartt

Translation by Ewert Cousins

Edited by Emilie Griffin

HarperOne
An Imprint of HarperCollinsPublishers

HarperOne

THE LIFE OF ST. FRANCIS. Original translation published by Paulist Press, 997 Macarthur Boulevard, Mahwah, NJ 07430; www.paulistpress.com. Copyright © 1978 by Paulist Press, Inc. Foreword © 2005 by Donna Tartt. All rights reserved. Printed in the United States of America. No part of this book may be used or reproduced in any manner whatsoever without written permission except in the case of brief quotations embodied in critical articles and reviews. For information, address HarperCollins Publishers, 195 Broadway, New York, NY 10007.

HarperCollins books may be purchased for educational, business, or sales promotional use. For information, please e-mail the Special Markets Department at SPsales@harpercollins.com

HarperCollins Web site: http://www.harpercollins.com

HarperCollins®, ♣®, and HarperOne™ are trademarks of HarperCollins Publishers.

Library of Congress Cataloging-in-Publication Data

Bonaventure, Saint, Cardinal, ca. 1217–1274.
   [Legenda maior S. Francisci. English]
   The life of St. Francis / Bonaventure ; foreword by Donna Tartt ; edited by Emilie Griffin ; translation by Ewert Cousins. — 1st ed.
     p. cm.
   ISBN 978-0-06-057652-3
   1. Francis, of Assisi, Saint, 1182–1226. I. Title: Life of Saint Francis. II. Griffin, Emilie. III. Cousins, Ewert H. IV. Title
BX4700.F65E5   2005
271'.302—dc22
[B]   2004059680

HB 04.27.2020

CONTENTS

FOREWORD

From the instant Francis Bernardone first stepped into the arms of the Bishop of Assisi and onto the field of history, he has been beloved by pagan and Christian alike. In fact, of all the saints, he is perhaps the greatest ambassador of the Church—the ideal introduction to Christianity for people of different faiths and cultures. And this is certainly because of Francis's great character and charm, but also because his message is far wider than the institutional Christianity of his day or our own: a faith so radiantly inclusive that it hails the birds as sisters, and addresses a cricket with as much reverence and courtesy as a bishop; a compassionate love that extends not only to all sentient beings, but to flowers and trees and the inanimate elements of heavenly creation: water and fire, sun and moon and stars.

Other saints—even very great ones—go in and out of fashion, or may not be recognized as saints until centuries after death. But Francis's popularity was unique and unprecedented in his own lifetime, and it has continued undiminished from his death in 1226 to the present day. We all know about the love St. Francis had for animals (and they for him) which marks him out distinctively from the times in which he lived, when even human life went cheap. But St. Francis's care for the poor and outcast members of society was was also quite radical in the feudal, hierarchical, aristocratic society of Medieval Europe; and his pacificm—hearkening back to Christ himself, and the very earliest teachings of Christianity—was nothing short of revolutionary. Indeed, as G.K.

Chesterton remarks, Francis "anticipated all that is most liberal and sympathetic in the modern mood; the love of nature; the love of animals, the sense of social compassion; the sense of the spiritual dangers of prosperity and even of property. All these things that nobody understood before Wordsworth were familiar to St. Francis."

Francis died young, while he was in his forties, and he was canonized only two years after his death, when St. Bonaventure, the author of this life (and a great saint in his own right) was eleven years old. Though Bonaventure probably was not acquainted with Francis personally, he attributes to Francis a miraculous cure from a boyhood illness, which suggests that Bonaventure may have seen Francis as a boy, or heard him speak on one of his preaching tours about Italy. And though Bonaventure relied most heavily on earlier accounts in compiling this life, he also spoke to a number of Francis's surviving contemporaries. The official portrait of St. Francis that subsequently emerges in these pages is not a history or a biography in the modern sense of the word, but neither is it a sentimental rendering of the familiar figure we know from cat tags and garden statuary. Rather, Bonaventure's anecdotes give a sharp sense of the living man himself. Francis is whimsical and affectionate and almost always in a hurry; he is quick to correct himself and assume blame when he thinks he is wrong; he is at once excessively polite and bewilderingly abrupt; he is often very funny; he is generous almost to lunacy. He is also a master of the dramatic gesture, and some of these gestures (such as his extreme aceticism and self-mortification) will be less congenial to modern readers than others. But it is important to remember that Francis—who was by no means an intellectual or an educated man—taught mainly by the example of his life, in an age when Pride—in the feudal aristocracy, in the hubris of the Crusades, in the pomp of the medieval church and the avarice of the growing merchant economy—was the major sin. If his insistence on poverty and humility seems extreme to us (if he was invited to a meal at a fine house, for instance, he would not eat what his hosts provided, but bring along instead a lowly meal he had begged along the way), we must always remember that Francis treated himself so harshly because he was so determined to give all his love and tenderness to creatures who needed it more than he did. There's never anything sour or grim about Francis's aceticism; what continually characterizes it is a warm spirit of open-handed gladness.

Indeed Francis—in his sweetness and strength, in his unswerving compassion for all beings—is very reminiscent of some of the great Buddhist saints and Boddhisatvas, but he is also probably the closest thing we have to a bhakti or a sufi in the Western tradition. He is wholly uninterested in the outer trappings of dogma and ritual; what matters to him is inner devotion, the life of the heart. And people from other religious traditions seem always to have seen this passionate inner holiness and to have recognized in him a friend and kinsman. In Chapter Nine, Bonaventure tells us that Francis, "armed with faith and not weapons," took it upon himself at the height of the Crusades to venture on a peaceful mission into Syria, at a time when the fighting was hot and the Soldan was offfering a gold piece to any Muslim who brought in the head of a Christian. But the Soldan was as taken with Francis as just about everyone else was who encountered him seems to have been. Instead of martyring Francis, he invited him to stay for a visit and—far from killing him—attemped to load him down with gifts; when Francis realized that the Soldan would not be converted, they parted amicably and he went back home.

For my part, I first became intrigued by St. Francis of Assissi when I was about fourteen years old, thanks to Zooey Glass's remark to Franny, in *Franny and Zooey*, that St. Francis was more loveable than Jesus. I didn't know anything about St. Francis, but the idea that the hyper-intellectual Glass siblings (whom I adored) found something "loveable" in the Christian faith made me intensely curious, since I—like the Soldan of Syria—was in those days resolutely hostile to Christianity and anything to do with it. Growing up in a part of America stringently dominated by Christian fundamentalism, and not being sympathetic to it by either upbringing or temperament, I had come to believe with all my ninth-grade heart that all Christianity everywhere (ancient, modern, Catholic, protestant) was as suffocating and humorless as the evangelical bullying which was for me a dispiriting fact of life. (Perhaps other children were edified to learn that working mothers were destined for hell fire, or by being forced to wear black yarn tied around a finger signifying that they were "against Christ," but I was not one of them). Consequently, I first came to these stories of Francis's life in a mood of defiance and hard-won suspicion—and, quite to my surprise, found myself captivated by a friendly, delightful spirit, very different from anything I'd ever encountered in Christianity. It was a change of heart both comical and appropriate, because if there's any atmosphere that defines Bonaventure's life, it's this playful element of reversal. Zooey was right: who can resist Francis? Francis who talked to pheasants and rabbits, Francis who invented the Christmas creche? Ecclesiastical opponents, man-eating wolves, enemies and hostile parties of every sort march forward to confront him—and all fall away (bemused, mollified, dumbfounded) before the cloth merchant's son that Chesterton rightly calls the court fool of the King of Paradise.

—DONNA TARTT

PROLOGUE

Here begins the prologue to the life of blessed Francis

In these last days
the grace of God our Savior has appeared
in his servant Francis
to all who are truly humble and lovers of holy
    poverty.
In him
they can venerate God's superabundant mercy
and be taught by his example
to utterly reject ungodliness and worldly
    passions,
to live in conformity with Christ
and to thirst after blessed hope with unflagging
    desire.
He was poor and lowly,
but the Most High God looked upon him
with such condescension and kindness
that he not only lifted him up in his need
from the dust of a worldly life,
but made him a practitioner, a leader and a
    herald
of Gospel perfection
and set him up as a light for believers
so that by bearing witness to the light
he might prepare for the Lord
a way of light and peace into the hearts of his
    faithful.

Shining with the splendor of his life and
    teaching,
like the morning star in the midst of clouds,
by his resplendent rays he guided into the light
those sitting in darkness and in the shadow of
    death,
and like the rainbow shining among clouds of
    glory
he made manifest in himself
the sign of the Lord's covenant.
He preached to men
the Gospel of peace and salvation,
being himself the Angel of true peace.
Like John the Baptist
he was appointed by God to prepare in the
    desert
a way of the highest poverty
and to preach repentance by word and
    example.
First endowed with the gifts of divine grace,
he was then enriched
by the merit of unshakable virtue;
and filled with the spirit of prophecy,
he was also assigned an angelic ministry
and was totally aflame with a Seraphic fire.
Like a hierarchic man
he was lifted up in a fiery chariot,
as will be seen quite clearly in the course of his
    life;
therefore it can be reasonably proved
that he came in the spirit and power of Elijah.

And so not without reason
is he considered to be symbolized by the image
   of the Angel
who ascends from the sunrise
bearing the seal of the living God,
in the true prophecy
of that other friend of the Bridegroom,
John the Apostle and Evangelist.
For "when the sixth seal was opened,"
John says in the Apocalypse,
"I saw another Angel
ascending from the rising of the sun,
having the seal of the living God."
   (Apoc. 6:12, 7:2)
We can come to the conclusion, without any
   doubt,
that this messenger of God—
so worthy to be loved by Christ,
imitated by us and admired by the world—
was God's servant Francis,
if we consider the height
of his extraordinary sanctity.
For even while he lived among men,
he imitated angelic purity
so that he was held up as an example
for those who would be perfect followers of
   Christ.
We are led to hold this firmly and devoutly
because of his ministry
to call men to weep and mourn,
to shave their heads, and to put on sackloth.

and to mark with a Tau
the foreheads of men who moan and grieve,
signing them with the cross of penance
and clothing them with his habit,
which is in the form of a cross.
But even more is this confirmed
with the irrefutable testimony of truth
by the seal of the likeness of the living God,
namely of Christ crucified,
which was imprinted on his body
not by natural forces or human skill
but by the wondrous power
of the Spirit of the living God.

I feel that I am unworthy and unequal to the task of writing the life of a man so venerable and worthy of imitation. I would never have attempted it if the fervent desire of the friars had not aroused me, the unanimous urging of the General Chapter had not induced me and the devotion which I am obliged to have toward our holy father had not compelled me. For when I was a boy, as I still vividly remember, I was snatched from the jaws of death by his invocation and merits. So if I remained silent and did not sing his praises, I fear that I would be rightly accused of the crime of ingratitude. I recognize that God saved my life through him, and I realize that I have experienced his power in my very person. This, then, is my principal reason for undertaking this task, that I may gather together the accounts of his virtues, his actions and his words—like so many fragments, partly forgotten and partly scattered—although I cannot accomplish this fully, so that they may not be lost (John 6:12) when those who lived with this servant of God die.

In order to have a clearer and more certain grasp of the authentic facts of his life, which I was to transmit to posterity, I visited the sites of the birth, life and death of this holy man. I had careful interviews with his companions who were still alive, especially those who had intimate knowledge of his holiness and were its principal followers. Because of their acknowledged truthfulness and their proven virtue, they can be trusted beyond any doubt. In describing what God graciously accomplished through his servant, I decided that I should avoid a cultivated literary style, since the reader's devotion profits more from simple rather than ornate expression. To avoid confusion I did not always weave the story together in chronological order. Rather, I strove to maintain a more thematic order, relating to the same theme events that happened at different times, and to different theme events that happened at the same time, as seemed appropriate.

Here ends the prologue

Chapter 1

On Saint Francis's Manner of Life While in Secular Attire

There was a man
in the town of Assisi,
Francis by name,
whose memory is held in benediction
because God in his generosity
foreordained goodly blessings for him,
mercifully snatching him from the dangers of
    the present life
and richly filling him with gifts of heavenly
    grace.
As a young boy,
he lived among worldly sons of men
and was brought up in worldly ways.
After acquiring
a little knowledge of reading and writing,
he was assigned
to work in a lucrative merchant's business.
Yet with God's protection,
even among wanton youths,
he did not give himself over
to the drives of the flesh,
although he indulged himself in pleasures;
nor even among greedy merchants
did he place his hope in money or treasures

>   although he was intent
>   on making a profit.

God implanted in the heart of the youthful Francis a certain openhanded compassion for the poor. Growing from his infancy, this compassion had so filled his heart with generosity that even at that time he determined not to be deaf to the Gospel but to give to everyone who begged, especially if he asked "for the love of God." On one occasion when Francis was distracted by the press of business, contrary to his custom, he sent away empty-handed a certain poor man who had begged alms for the love of God. As soon as he came to his senses, he ran after the man and gave him a generous alms, promising God that from that moment onward, while he had the means, he would never refuse those who begged from him for the love of God. He kept this promise with untiring fidelity until his death and merited an abundant increase of grace and love for God. Afterwards, when he had perfectly put on Christ, he used to say that even while he was in secular attire, he could scarcely ever hear any mention of the love of God without being deeply moved in his heart.

His gentleness, his refined manners, his patience, his superhuman affability, his generosity beyond his means, marked him as a young man of flourishing natural disposition. This seemed to be a prelude to the even greater abundance of God's blessings that would be showered on him in the future. Indeed a certain man of Assisi, an exceptionally simple fellow who, it is believed, was inspired by God, whenever he chanced to meet Francis going through the town, used to take off his cloak and spread it under his feet saying that Francis deserved every sign of respect since he was destined to do great things in the near future and would be magnificently honored by the entire body of the faithful.

Up to this time, however, Francis was ignorant of God's plan for him. He was distracted by the external affairs of his father's business and drawn down toward earthly things by the corruption of human nature. As a result, he had not yet learned how to contemplate the things of heaven nor had he acquired a taste for the things of God. Since affliction can enlighten our spiritual awareness, the hand of the Lord came upon him, and the right hand of God effected a change in him. God afflicted his body with a prolonged illness in order to prepare his soul for the anointing of the Holy Spirit. After his strength was restored, when he had dressed as usual in his fine clothes, he met a certain knight who was of noble birth, but poor and badly clothed. Moved to compassion for his poverty, Francis took off his own garments and clothed the man on the spot. At one and the same time he fulfilled the twofold duty of covering over the embarrassment of a noble knight and relieving the poverty of a poor man.

The following night, when he had fallen asleep, God in his goodness showed him a large and splendid palace full of military weapons emblazoned with the insignia of Christ's cross. Thus God vividly indicated that the compassion he had exhibited toward the poor knight for love of the supreme King would be repaid with an incomparable reward. And so when Francis asked to whom these belonged, he received an answer from heaven that all these things were for him and his knights. When he awoke in the morning, he judged the strange vision to be an indication that he would have great prosperity; for he had no experience in interpreting divine mysteries nor did he know how to pass through visible images to grasp the invisible truth beyond. Therefore, still ignorant of God's plan, he decided to join a certain count in Apulia, hoping in his service to obtain the glory of knighthood, as his vision seemed to foretell.

He set out on his journey shortly afterwards; but when he had gone as far as the next town, he heard during the night the Lord address him in a familiar way, saying: "Francis, who can do more for you, a lord or a servant, a rich man or a poor man?" When Francis replied that a lord and a rich man could do more, he was at once asked: "Why, then, are you abandoning the Lord for a servant and the rich God for a poor man?" And Francis replied: "Lord, what will you have me do?" And the Lord answered him: "Return to your own land, because the vision which you have seen foretells a spiritual outcome which will be accomplished in you not by human but by divine planning." In the morning, then, he returned in haste to Assisi, joyous and free of care; already a model of obedience, he awaited the Lord's will.

From that time on he withdrew from the bustle of public business and devoutly begged God in his goodness to show him what he should do. The flame of heavenly desire was fanned in him by his frequent prayer, and his desire for his heavenly home led him to despise as nothing all earthly things. He realized that he had found a hidden treasure, and like the wise merchant he planned to sell all he had and to buy the pearl he had found (Matt. 13:44–46). Nevertheless, how he should do this, he did not yet know; but it was being suggested to him inwardly that to be a spiritual merchant one must begin with contempt for the world and to be a knight of Christ one must begin with victory over one's self.

One day while he was riding on horseback through the plain that lies below the town of Assisi, he came upon a leper. This unforeseen encounter struck him with horror. But he recalled his resolution to be perfect and remembered that he must first conquer himself if he wanted to become a knight of Christ. He slipped off his horse and ran to kiss the man. When the leper put out his hand as if to receive some alms, Francis gave him money and a kiss. Immediately mounting his horse, Francis looked all around; but although the open plain stretched clear in all directions, he could not see the leper anywhere. Filled with wonder and joy, he began devoutly to sing God's praises, resolving from this always to strive to do greater things in the future.

After that he began to seek out solitary places, well suited for sorrow; and there he prayed incessantly with unutterable groanings. After long and urgent prayer, he merited to be heard by the Lord. One day while he was praying in such a secluded spot and became totally absorbed in God through his extreme fervor, Jesus Christ appeared to him fastened to the cross. Francis's soul melted at the sight, and the memory of Christ's passion was so impressed on the innermost recesses of his heart that from that hour, whenever Christ's crucifixion came to his mind, he could scarcely contain his tears and sighs, as he later revealed to his companions when he was approaching the end of his life. Through this the man of God understood as addressed to himself the Gospel text: "If you wish to come after me, deny yourself and take up your cross and follow me" (Matt. 16:24).

From that time on he clothed himself with a spirit of poverty, a sense of humility and a feeling of intimate devotion. Formerly he used to be horrified not only by close dealing with lepers but by their very sight, even from a distance; but now he rendered humble service to the lepers with human concern and devoted kindness in order that he might completely despise himself, because of Christ crucified, who according to the text of the prophet was despised as a leper (Isa. 53:3). He visited their houses frequently, generously distributed alms to them and with great compassion kissed their hands and their mouths.

To beggars he wished to give not only his possessions but his very self. At times he took off his clothes, at times unstitched them, at times ripped them in pieces, in order to give them to beggars, when he had nothing else at hand. He came to the assistance of poor priests, reverently and devoutly, especially in adorning the altar. In this way he became a participator in the divine worship, while supplying the needs of its celebrants. During this period of time he made a pilgrimage to the shrine of St. Peter, where he saw a large number of the poor before the entrance of the church. Led partly by the sweetness of his devotion, partly by the love of poverty, he gave his own clothes to one of the neediest among them. Then he dressed in the poor man's rags and spent that day in the midst of the poor with an unaccustomed joy of spirit. This he did in order to spurn worldly glory and, by ascending in stages, to arrive at the perfection of the Gospel.

> He paid great attention
> to the mortification of the flesh
> so that he might carry externally in his body
> the cross of Christ
> which he carried internally in his heart.
> Francis, the man of God,
> did all these things
> when he was not yet withdrawn
> from the dress and life of the world.

Chapter 2

On His Perfect Conversion to God and His Restoration of Three Churches

Francis,
the servant of the Most High,
had no other teacher in these matters
except Christ,
whose kindness was shown once more
by visiting him with the sweetness of grace.

One day when Francis went out to meditate in the fields, he walked beside the church of San Damiano, which was threatening to collapse because of extreme age. Inspired by the Spirit, he went inside to pray. Prostrate before an image of the Crucified, he was filled with no little consolation as he prayed. While his tear-filled eyes were gazing at the Lord's cross, he heard with his bodily ears a voice coming from the cross, telling him three times: "Francis, go and repair my house, which, as you see, is falling completely into ruin."

Trembling with fear, Francis was amazed at the sound of this astonishing voice, since he was alone in the church; and as he received in his heart the power of the divine words, he fell into a state of ecstasy. Returning finally to his senses, he prepared to obey, gathering himself together to carry out the command of repairing the church materially, although the principal intention of the words referred to that Church which "Christ purchased with his own blood" (Acts 20:28), as the Holy Spirit taught him and as he himself later disclosed to the friars.

He rose then, made the sign of the cross, and taking some cloth to sell, hurried off to the town called Foligno. There he sold all he had brought with him, and, lucky merchant that he was, even sold the horse he was riding. Returning to Assisi, he reverently entered the church which he had been commanded to repair. When he found the poor priest there, he greeted him with fitting reverence, offered him money for the repairs on the church and for the poor, and humbly requested that the priest allow him to stay with him for a time. The priest agreed to his staying there but would not accept the money out of fear of his parents. True despiser of money that he was, Francis threw it on a window sill, valuing it no more than if it were dust.

When his father learned that the servant of God was staying with this priest, he was greatly disturbed and ran to the place. But Francis, upon hearing about the threats of those who were pursuing him and having a premonition that they were approaching, wished to "give place to wrath" (Rom. 12:19), and hid himself—being still untrained as an athlete of Christ—in a secret pit. There he remained in hiding for some days, imploring the Lord incessantly with a flood of tears to deliver him from the hands of those who were persecuting his soul and in his kindness to bring to realization the pious desires he had inspired. He was then filled with excessive joy and began to accuse himself of cowardice. He cast aside his fear, left the pit and took the road to the town of Assisi. When the townspeople saw his unkempt face and his changed mentality, they thought that he had gone out of his senses. They threw filth from the streets and stones at him, shouting insults at him, as if he were insane and out of his mind. But the Lord's servant passed through it as if he were deaf to it all, unbroken and unchanged by any of these insults. When his father heard the shouting, he ran to him at once, not to save him but to destroy him. Casting aside all compassion, he dragged him home, tormenting him first with words, then with blows and chains. But this made Francis all the more eager and stronger to carry out what he had begun, as he recalled the words of the Gospel: "Blessed are they who suffer persecution for justice's sake, for theirs is the kingdom of heaven" (Matt. 5:10).

After a little while, when his father went out of the country, his mother, who did not approve what her husband had done and had no hope of being able to soften her son's inflexible constancy, released him from his chains and permitted him to go away. He gave thanks to Almighty God and went back to the place where he had been before. Returning and not finding him at home, his father violently reproached his wife and in rage ran to that place. If he could not bring Francis back home, he would at least drive him out of the district. But strengthened by God, Francis went out on his own accord to meet his furious father, calling out in a clear voice that he cared nothing for his chains and blows. Besides, he stated that he would gladly undergo any evil for the name of Christ. When his father, therefore, saw that he could not bring him around, he turned his attention to getting his money back. When he finally found it thrown on the window sill, his rage was mitigated a little, and the thirst of his avarice was somewhat alleviated by the draft of money.

Thereupon his carnally minded father led this child of grace, now stripped of his money, before the bishop of the town. He wanted to have Francis renounce into his hands his family possessions and return everything he had. A true lover of poverty, Francis showed himself eager to comply; he went before the bishop without delaying or hesitating. He did not wait for any words nor did he speak any, but immediately took off his clothes and gave them back to his father. Then it was discovered that the man of God had a hairshirt next to his skin under his fine clothes. Moreover, drunk with remarkable fervor, he even took off his underwear, stripping himself completely naked before all. He said to his father: "Until now I have called you father here on earth, but now I can say without reservation, 'Our Father who art in heaven' (Matt. 6:9), since I have placed all my treasure and all my hope in him." When the bishop saw this, he was amazed at such intense fervor in the man of God. He immediately stood up and in tears drew Francis into his arms, covering him with the mantle he was wearing, like the pious and good man that he was. He bade his servants give Francis something to cover his body. They brought him a poor, cheap cloak of a farmer who worked for the bishop. Francis accepted it gratefully and with his own hand marked a cross on it with a piece of chalk, thus designating it as the covering of a crucified man and a half-naked beggar.

Thus the servant of the Most High King
was left naked
so that he might follow
his naked crucified Lord, whom he loved.
Thus the cross strengthened him
to entrust his soul
to the wood of salvation
that would save him from the shipwreck of
    the world.

Released now from the chains of all earthly desires, this despiser of the world left the town and in a carefree mood sought out a hidden place of solitude where alone and in silence he could hear the secrets God would convey to him. While Francis, the man of God, was making his way through a certain forest, merrily singing praises to the Lord in the French language, robbers suddenly rushed upon him from an ambush. When they asked in a brutal way who he was, the man of God, filled with confidence, replied with these prophetic words: "I am the herald of the great King." But they struck him and hurled him into a ditch filled with snow, saying: "Lie there, you hick herald of God!" When they went away, he jumped out of the ditch, and brimming over with joy, in a loud voice began to make the forest resound with the praises of the Creator of all.

Coming to a certain neighboring monastery, he asked for alms like a beggar and received it—unrecognized and subjected to contempt. Setting out from there, he came to Gubbio, where he was recognized and welcomed by a former friend and given a poor little tunic, like one of Christ's little poor. From there the lover of complete humility went to the lepers and lived with them, serving them all most diligently for God's sake. He washed their feet, bandaged their ulcers, drew the pus from their wounds and washed out the diseased matter; he even kissed their ulcerous wounds out of his remarkable devotion, he who was soon to be a physician of the Gospel. As a result, he received such power from the Lord that he had miraculous effectiveness in healing spiritual and physical illnesses. I will cite one case among many, which occurred after the fame of the man of God became more widely known. There was a man in the vicinity of Spoleto whose mouth and cheek were being eaten away by a certain horrible disease. He could not be helped by any medical treatment and went on a pilgrimage to implore the intercession of the holy apostles. On his way back from visiting their shrines, he happened to meet God's servant. When out of devotion he wanted to kiss Francis's footprints, that humble man, refusing to allow it, kissed the mouth of the one who wished to kiss his feet. In his remarkable compassion Francis, the servant of lepers, touched that horrible sore with his holy mouth, and suddenly every sign of the disease vanished and the sick man recovered the health he longed for. I do not know which of these we should admire more: the depth of his humility in such a compassionate kiss or his extraordinary power in such an amazing miracle.

Grounded now in the humility of Christ, Francis recalled to mind the command enjoined upon him from the cross, to repair the church of San Damiano. As a truly obedient man, he returned to Assisi to obey the divine command at least by begging aid. Putting aside all embarrassment out of love of Christ's poor and crucified, he begged from those among whom he used to show his wealth, and he loaded stones upon his body that was weakened by fasting. With God's help and the devoted assistance of the citizens, he completed repairs on the church. After this work, to prevent his body from becoming sluggish with laziness, he set himself to repair a certain church of St. Peter some distance from the town, because of the special devotion which, in his pure and sincere faith, he bore to the prince of the apostles.

When he finally completed this church, he came to a place called the Portiuncula where there was a church dedicated to the Blessed Virgin Mother of God, built in ancient times but now deserted and cared for by no one. When the man of God saw how it was abandoned, he began to live there in order to repair it, moved by the fervent devotion he had toward the Lady of the world. According to the name of the church, which since ancient times was called St. Mary of the Angels, he felt that angels often visited there. So he took up residence there out of his reverence for the angels and his special love for the mother of Christ. The holy man loved this spot more than any other in the world. For here he began humbly, here he progressed steadily, here he ended happily. At his death he commended it to the friars as a place most dear to the Virgin.

Before his conversion, a certain friar, devoted to God, had a vision about this church which is worth relating. He saw a large group of men who had been struck blind, kneeling in a circle about this church, their faces turned to heaven. With uplifted hands and tearful voices, they were crying out to God, begging that he have pity on them and grant them sight. And behold, a splendrous light came down from heaven and spread over them all, giving to each his sight and the health they had longed for.

This is the place
where the Order of Friars Minor was begun
by Saint Francis
under the inspiration of divine revelation.
For at the bidding of divine providence
which guided Christ's servant in everything,
he physically repaired three churches
before he began the Order
and preached the Gospel.
This he did
not only
to ascend in an orderly progression
from the sensible realm to the intelligible,
from the lesser to the greater,
but also
to symbolize prophetically
in external actions perceived by the senses
what he would do in the future.
For like the three buildings he repaired,
so Christ's Church—
with its threefold victorious army
of those who are to be saved—
was to be renewed under his leadership

in three ways:
by the structure, rule and teaching
which he would provide.
And now we see
that this prophecy has been fulfilled.

Chapter 3

On the Foundation of the Order and the Approval of the Rule

While her servant Francis
was living in the church of the Virgin Mother
    of God,
he prayed to her
who had conceived the Word full of grace and
    truth,
imploring her with continuous sighs
to become his advocate.
Through the merits
of the Mother of Mercy,
he conceived and brought to birth
the spirit of the truth of the Gospel.

One day when he was devoutly hearing a Mass of the Apostles, the Gospel was read in which Christ sends forth his disciples to preach and explains to them the way of life according to the Gospel: that they "should not keep gold or silver or money in their belts, nor have a wallet for their journey, nor two tunics, nor shoes, nor staff" (Matt. 10:9–10). When he heard this, he grasped its meaning and committed it to memory. This lover of apostolic poverty was then filled with an indescribable joy and said: "This is what I want; this is what I long for with all my heart." He immediately took off his shoes from his feet, put aside his staff, cast away his wallet and money as if accursed, was content with one tunic and exchanged his leather belt for a piece of rope. He directed all his heart's desire to carry out what he had heard and to conform in every way to the rule of right living given to the apostles.

Under divine inspiration the man of God now began to strive after Gospel perfection and invite others to penance. His words were not empty or joking, but full of the power of the Holy Spirit; they penetrated to the innermost depths of the heart, causing his hearers to be filled with amazement. In all his preaching, he proclaimed peace, saying: "May the Lord give you peace," as the greeting to the people at the beginning of his sermon. As he later testified, he had learned this greeting in a revelation from the Lord. Hence, according to the words of a prophet and inspired by the spirit of the prophets, he proclaimed peace, preached salvation and by his salutary warnings united in a bond of true peace many who had previously been in opposition to Christ and far from salvation.

When the truth of his simple teaching and his way of life became widely known, certain men began to be inspired to live a life of penance. Leaving everything, they joined him in his way of life and dress. The first among these was Bernard, a venerable man, who was made a sharer in a divine vocation and merited to be the firstborn son of our blessed father, both in priority of time and in the gift of holiness. When he discovered for himself the holiness of Christ's servant and decided to despise the world completely after his example, he sought his advice on how to carry this out. On hearing this, God's servant was filled with the consolation of the Holy Spirit over the conception of his first child. "We must ask God's advice about this," he said. In the morning they went to the church of St. Nicholas, where they said some preliminary prayers; then Francis, who was devoted to the Trinity, opened the book of the Gospel three times, asking God to confirm Bernard's plan with a threefold testimony. The book opened the first time to the text: "If you will be perfect, go, sell all that you have, and give to the poor" (Matt. 19:21). The second time to the text: "Take nothing on your journey" (Luke 9:3). And the third time to: "If anyone wishes to come after me, let him deny himself and take up his cross and follow me" (Matt. 16:24). "This is our life and our rule," the holy man said, "and the life and the rule of all who wish to join our company. Go, then, if you wish to be perfect and carry out what you have heard."

Not long afterwards five other men were called by the same Spirit, and the number of Francis's sons reached six. The third among them was the holy father Giles, a man indeed filled with God and worthy of his celebrated reputation. Although he was a simple and unlearned man, he later became famous for his practice of heroic virtue, as God's servant had prophesied, and was raised to the height of exalted contemplation. For through the passage of many years, he strove without ceasing to direct himself toward God; and he was so often rapt into God in ecstasy, as I myself have observed as an eyewitness, that he seemed to live among men more like an angel than a human being.

Also at that time a certain priest of the town of Assisi, named Silvester, an upright man, was shown a vision by the Lord which should not be passed over in silence. Reacting in a purely human way, he had developed an abhorrence for the way Francis and his friars were going. But then he was visited by grace from heaven in order to save him from the danger of rash judgment. For he saw in a dream the whole town of Assisi encircled by a huge dragon which threatened to destroy the entire area by its enormous size. Then he saw coming from Francis's mouth a golden cross whose top touched heaven and whose arms stretched far and wide and seemed to extend to the ends of the world. At the sight of its shining splendor, the foul and hideous dragon was put to flight. When he had seen this vision for the third time and realized that it was a divine revelation, he told it point by point to the man of God and his friars. Not long afterwards he left the world and followed in the footsteps of Christ with such perseverance that his life in the Order confirmed the authenticity of the vision which he had had in the world.

On hearing of this vision, the man of God was not carried away by human glory; but recognizing God's goodness in his gifts, was more strongly inspired to put to flight our ancient enemy with his cunning and to preach the glory of the cross of Christ. One day while he was weeping as he looked back over his past years in bitterness, the joy of the Holy Spirit came over him and he was assured that all of his sins had been completely forgiven. Then he was rapt in ecstasy and totally absorbed in a wonderful light, his heart was expanded and he clearly saw what would transpire for him and his sons in the future. After this he returned to the friars and said: "Take strength, my beloved ones, and rejoice in the Lord. Do not be sad because you are few in number, nor afraid because of my simplicity or yours. For as the Lord has shown me in truth, God will make us grow into a great multitude and will cause us to expand in countless ways by the grace of his blessing."

At the same time, another good man entered the Order, bringing the number of Francis's sons to seven. Then like a devoted father, Francis gathered all his sons around him and explained to them many things concerning the kingdom of God, contempt for the world, the renunciation of their own wills and the mortification of their bodies. Then he disclosed to them his plan to send them to the four corners of the world. For already the lowly and seemingly sterile simplicity of our holy father had brought to birth seven sons. And now he wished to call all the faithful of the world to repentance and to bring them to birth in Christ the Lord. "Go," said the gentle father to his sons, "proclaim peace to men and preach repentance for the forgiveness of sins. Be patient in trials, watchful in prayer, strenuous in work, moderate in speech, reserved in manner and grateful for favors, because for all this an eternal kingdom is being prepared for you." The friars humbly cast themselves on the ground before God's servant and received the command of obedience in a spirit of joy. Then he said to each one of them individually: "Cast your care upon the Lord and he will support you" (Ps. 55:22). This is what he used to say whenever he sent a friar somewhere under obedience.

Francis knew he should give an example to others and wanted to practice what he preached; so he himself set out in one direction with one of his companions. The remaining six he sent in the other three directions, thus forming the pattern of a cross. After a short time had passed, the loving father longed for the presence of his dear children; and since he could not summon them himself, he prayed that this should be done by God, who gathers together the dispersed of Israel. It happened that, just as he wished, they all came together shortly afterwards quite unexpectedly and much to their surprise, through the kindness of divine providence, without being summoned in any human way. During those days four upright men joined them, increasing their number to twelve.

Seeing that the number of friars was gradually increasing, Christ's servant wrote in simple words a rule of life for himself and his friars. He based it on the unshakable foundation of the observance of the Gospel and added a few other things that seemed necessary for their way of life in common. He very much wanted to have what he had written approved by the Supreme Pontiff; so he decided to go with his band of simple men before the presence of the Apostolic See, placing his trust solely in God's guidance. From on high God looked with favor upon his desire and comforted the souls of his companions who were frightened at the thought of their simplicity, by showing him the following vision. It seemed to him that he was walking along a certain road beside which stood a very tall tree. Drawing near, he stood under it and marveled at its height. Suddenly he was lifted up by divine power to such a height that he was able to touch the top of the tree and very easily bend it down to the ground. Filled with God, he realized that the vision was a prophecy of how the Apostolic See, with all its dignity, would show him condescension; and he was overjoyed. He encouraged his friars in the Lord and set out with them on the journey.

When he arrived in Rome, he was led into the presence of the Supreme Pontiff. The Vicar of Christ was in the Lateran Palace, walking in a place called the Hall of the Mirror, occupied in deep meditation. Knowing nothing of Christ's servant, he sent him away indignantly. Francis left humbly, and the next night God showed the Supreme Pontiff the following vision. He saw a palm tree sprout between his feet and grow gradually until it became a beautiful tree. As he wondered what this vision might mean, the divine light impressed upon the mind of the Vicar of Christ that this palm tree symbolized the poor man whom he had sent away the previous day. The next morning he commanded his servants to search the city for the poor man. When they found him near the Lateran at St. Anthony's hospice, he ordered him brought to his presence without delay.

When he was led before the Supreme Pontiff, Francis explained his plan, humbly and urgently imploring him to approve the rule of life mentioned before. Now the Vicar of Christ, Innocent III, was a man famous for his wisdom; and when he saw in the man of God such remarkable purity and simplicity of heart, such firmness of purpose and such fiery ardor of will, he was inclined to give his assent to the request. Yet he hesitated to do what Christ's little poor man asked because it seemed to some of the cardinals to be something novel and difficult beyond human powers. There was among the cardinals a most venerable man, John of St. Paul, bishop of Sabina, a lover of holiness and helper of Christ's poor. Inspired by the Holy Spirit, he said to the Supreme Pontiff and his brother cardinals: "If we refuse the request of this poor man as novel or too difficult, when all he asks is to be allowed to lead the Gospel life, we must be on our guard lest we commit an offense against Christ's Gospel. For if anyone says that there is something novel or irrational or impossible to observe in this man's desire to live according to the perfection of the Gospel, he is guilty of blasphemy against Christ, the author of the Gospel." At this observation, the successor of the Apostle Peter turned to the poor man of Christ and said: "My son, pray to Christ that he may show us his will through you. When we know this with more certainty, we can give our approval to your pious desires with more assurance."

The servant of Almighty God totally gave himself to prayer, and through his devout supplications obtained for himself knowledge of what he should say outwardly and for the pope what he should think inwardly. Francis told the pope a parable, which he had learned from God, about a rich king who voluntarily married a poor but beautiful woman. She bore him children who resembled the king and for this reason could be brought up at his table. Then Francis added by way of interpretation: "The sons and heirs of the eternal King should not fear that they will die of hunger. They have been born of a poor mother by the power of the Holy Spirit in the image of Christ the King, and they will be begotten by the spirit of poverty in our poor little Order. For if the King of heaven promises his followers an eternal kingdom, he will certainly supply them with those things that he gives to the good and the bad alike." When the Vicar of Christ had listened to this parable and its interpretation, he was quite amazed and recognized without the slightest doubt that here Christ had spoken through man. And he affirmed that a vision which he had recently received from heaven through the inspiration of the divine Spirit would be fulfilled in this man. He had seen in a dream, as he recounted, that a little poor man, insignificant and despised, was holding up on his back the Lateran basilica, which was about to collapse. "This is certainly the man," he said, "who by his work and teaching will hold up the Church of Christ." Filled with reverence for Francis, he was favorably inclined toward everything he asked and always held Christ's servant in special affection. Then he granted what was requested and promised to grant even more in the future. He approved the rule and gave them a mission to preach penance, and he had small tonsures shaved on the laymen among Francis's companions so that they could freely preach the word of God.

Chapter 4

On the Progress of the Order under His Hand and the Confirmation of the Rule

Strengthened by God's grace and the pope's approval, Francis with great confidence took the road toward the valley of Spoleto, where he intended to preach and to live the Gospel of Christ. On the way he discussed with his companions how they should sincerely keep the rule which they had taken upon themselves, how they should proceed in all holiness and justice before God, how they should improve themselves and be an example for others. It was already late in the day as they continued their long discussion. Fatigued from their prolonged activity and feeling hungry, they stopped at an isolated spot. When there seemed to be no way for them to get the food they needed, God's providence immediately came to their aid. For suddenly a man appeared carrying bread in his hand, which he gave to Christ's little poor, and then suddenly disappeared. They had no idea where he came from or where he went. From this the poor friars realized that while in the company of the man of God they would be given assistance from heaven, and so they were refreshed more by the gift of God's generosity than by the food they had received for their bodies. Moreover, filled with divine consolation, they firmly resolved and irrevocably committed themselves never to turn back from the promise they had made to holy poverty, in spite of any pressure from lack of food or other trials.

When they arrived at the valley of Spoleto full of their holy plans, they began to discuss whether they should live among the people or go off into places of solitude. But Christ's servant Francis did not place his trust in his own efforts or those of his companions; rather he sought to discern God's will in this matter by earnest prayer. Then, enlightened by a revelation from heaven, he realized that he was sent by the Lord to win for Christ the souls which the devil was trying to snatch away. Therefore he chose to live for all men rather than for himself alone, drawn by the example of the one who deigned to die for all.

Then with his companions the man of God took shelter in an abandoned hut near the town of Assisi, where they barely subsisted according to the rule of holy poverty in much labor and want, drawing their nourishment more from the bread of tears than from the delights of bodily food. They spent their time there praying incessantly, devoting themselves to mental rather than vocal prayer because they did not yet have liturgical books from which to chant the canonical hours. In place of these they had the book of Christ's cross, which they studied continually day and night, taught by the example and words of their father who spoke to them constantly about the cross of Christ. When the friars asked him to teach them to pray, he said: "When you pray, say 'Our Father. . .' and 'We adore you, O Christ, in all your churches in the whole world, and we bless you because by your holy cross

you have redeemed the world.'" He also taught them to praise
God in all creatures and from all creatures, to honor priests with
special reverence and to firmly believe and simply profess the true
faith as held and taught by the Holy Roman Church. The friars
followed his teaching in every detail; and before every church
and crucifix which they saw, even from a distance, they humbly
prostrated themselves and prayed according to the form he had
taught them.

While the friars were still staying in the place already mentioned, one Saturday the holy man went to the town of Assisi to
preach in the cathedral on Sunday morning, as was his custom.
The devoted man of God spent the night in prayer, as he usually
did, in a hut situated in the garden of the canons, separated physically from the friars. At about midnight while some of the friars
were resting and others continued to pray, behold, a fiery chariot
of wonderful brilliance entered through the door of the house and
turned here and there three times through the house. A globe of
light rested above it which shone like the sun and lit up the night.
Those who were awake were dumbfounded, and those who were
sleeping woke up terrified. They felt the brightness light up their
hearts no less than their bodies, and the conscience of each was
laid bare to the others by the strength of that marvelous light. As
they looked into each other's hearts, they all realized together that
their holy father, who was absent physically, was present in spirit,
transfigured in this image. And they realized that by supernatural
power the Lord had shown him to them in this glowing chariot of
fire, radiant with heavenly splendor and inflamed with burning
ardor so that they might follow him like true Israelites. Like a sec-

ond Elijah, God had made him a chariot and charioteer for spiritual men. Certainly we can believe that God opened the eyes of these simple men at the prayers of Francis so that they might see the wonders of God just as he had once opened the eyes of the servant of Elisha so that he could see "the mountain full of horses and chariots of fire round about the prophet" (2 Kings 6:17). When the holy man returned to the friars, he began to probe the secrets of their consciences, to draw courage for them from this wonderful vision and to make many predictions about the growth of the Order. When he disclosed many things that transcended human understanding, the friars realized the Spirit of the Lord had come to rest upon him in such fullness that it was absolutely safe for them to follow his life and teaching.

After this, under the guidance of heavenly grace, the shepherd Francis led the little flock of twelve friars to St. Mary of the Portiuncula, so that there, where the Order of Friars Minor had had its beginning by the merits of the mother of God, it might also begin to grow with her assistance. There, also, he became a herald of the Gospel. He went about the towns and villages proclaiming the kingdom of God not in words taught by human wisdom, but in the power of the Spirit. To those who saw him, he seemed to be a man of another world as, with his mind and face always turned toward heaven, he tried to draw them all on high. As a result, the vineyard of Christ began to sprout shoots with the fragrance of the Lord and to bring forth abundant fruit, producing blossoms of sweetness, of honor and goodness.

Set on fire by the fervor of his preaching, a great number of people bound themselves by new laws of penance according to the rule which they received from the man of God. Christ's servant decided to name this way of life the Order of the Brothers of Penance. As the road of penance is common to all who are striving toward heaven, so this way of life admits clerics and laity, single and married of both sexes. How meritorious it is before God is clear from the numerous miracles performed by some of its members. Young women, too, were drawn to perpetual celibacy, among whom was the maiden Clare, who was especially dear to God.

> She was the first tender sprout
> among these
> and gave forth fragrance
> like a bright white flower
> that blossoms in springtime,
> and she shone
> like a radiant star.
> Now she is glorified
> in heaven
> and venerated in a fitting manner
> by the Church on earth,
> she who was the daughter in Christ
> of our holy father Francis, the little poor man,
> and the mother of the Poor Clares.

Many people also, not only stirred by devotion but inflamed by a desire for the perfection of Christ, despised the emptiness of worldly things and followed in the footsteps of Francis. Their numbers increased daily and quickly reached to the ends of the earth.

Holy poverty,
which was all they had to meet their expenses,
made them prompt for obedience,
robust for work and free for travel.
Because they possessed nothing that belonged
    to the world,
they were attached to nothing and feared to
    lose nothing.
They were safe everywhere,
not held back by fear, nor distracted by care;
they lived with untroubled minds,
and, without any anxiety,
looked forward to the morrow
and to finding a lodging for the night.
In different parts of the world
many insults were hurled against them
as persons unknown and despised.
But their love of the Gospel of Christ
had made them so patient
that they sought
to be where they would suffer physical persecution
rather than where their holiness was recognized
and they could glory in worldly honor.
Their very poverty
seemed to them overflowing abundance
since, according to the advice of the wise man,
they were content with a minimum
as if it were much.

When some of the friars went to the lands of the infidels, a certain Saracen, moved by compassion, once offered them money

for the food they needed. When they refused to accept it the man was amazed, seeing that they were without means. Realizing they did not want to possess money because they had become poor out of love of God, he felt so attracted to them that he offered to provide for their needs as long as he had something to give.

> O inestimable value of poverty,
> whose marvelous power moved
> the fierce heart of a barbarian
> to such sweet compassion!
> What a horrible and unspeakable crime
> that a Christian should trample underfoot
> this noble pearl
> which a Saracen held in such veneration!

At that time a certain religious of the Order of the Crosiers, Morico by name, was suffering from such a grave and prolonged illness in a hospital near Assisi that the doctors had already despaired of his life. In his need, he turned to the man of God, urgently entreating him through a messenger to intercede for him before the Lord. Our blessed father kindly consented and said a prayer for him. Then he took some bread crumbs and mixed them with oil taken from a lamp that burned before the altar of the Virgin. He made a kind of pill out of them and sent it to the sick man through the hands of the friars, saying: "Take this medicine to our brother Morico. By means of it Christ's power will not only restore him to full health but will make him a sturdy warrior and enlist him in our forces permanently." When the sick man took the medicine which had been prepared under the inspiration of the Holy Spirit, he was cured immediately. God gave him such strength of mind and body that when a little later he entered the holy man's Order, he wore only a single tunic, under which for a long time he wore a hairshirt next to his skin. He was satisfied with uncooked food such as herbs, vegetables and fruit and for many years never tasted bread or wine, yet remained strong and in good health.

As the merits of virtue increased in Christ's little poor men, their good reputation spread all about and attracted a great number of people from different parts of the world to come and see our holy father. Among them was a spirited composer of worldly songs, who had been crowned by the Emperor and was therefore called the King of Verses. He decided to visit the man of God, who despised the things of the world. When he found him preaching in a monastery in the village of San Severino, the hand of the Lord came upon him; and he saw Francis, the preacher of Christ's cross, signed with a cross, in the form of two flashing swords, one of which stretched from his head to his feet, the other crossed his chest from one hand to the other. He did not know Christ's servant by sight, but quickly recognized him once he had been pointed out by so great a miracle. Dumbfounded at the vision, he immediately began to resolve to do better. He was struck in his conscience by the power of the saint's words, as if pierced by a spiritual sword coming from his mouth. He completely despised his worldly popularity and joined our blessed father by making a religious profession. When the holy man saw that he had been completely converted from the restlessness of the world to the peace of Christ, he called him Brother Pacificus. Afterwards he advanced in holiness; and before he went to France as provincial minister—indeed he was the first to hold that office there—he merited to see a second vision: a great Tau on Francis's forehead, which shone in a variety of colors and caused his face to glow with wonderful beauty. The holy man venerated this symbol with great affection, often spoke highly of it and signed it with his own hand at the end of the letters which he sent, as if his whole desire were to mark with a Tau the foreheads of men who have been truly converted to Jesus Christ and "who moan and grieve," according to the text of the Prophet (Ezek. 9:4).

As the number of friars increased with the passing of time, Francis began to summon them, like a solicitous shepherd, to a general chapter at St. Mary of the Portiuncula, so as to allot to each a portion of obedience in the land of their poverty, according to the measuring-cord of divine distribution. Although there was a complete lack of all necessities and sometimes the friars numbered more than five thousand, nevertheless with the assistance of divine mercy, they had adequate food, enjoyed physical health and overflowed with spiritual joy.

Francis could not be physically present at the provincial chapters, but he was present in spirit through his solicitous care in governing, his insistent prayers and his effective blessing. Occasionally, however, he did appear visibly by God's miraculous power. For at the chapter of Arles that outstanding preacher Anthony, who is now a glorious confessor of Christ, was preaching to the friars on the inscription on the cross: "Jesus of Nazareth, King of the Jews" (John 19:19). A certain friar of proven virtue, Monaldus by name, was moved by divine inspiration to look toward the door of the chapter and saw with his bodily eyes blessed Francis lifted up in midair, his arms extended as though on a cross, and blessing the friars. All the friars felt themselves filled with such unusual inner consolation that it was clear the Spirit was giving them certain testimony that their holy father had been really present. In addition to these evident signs, it was later confirmed by the external testimony of the words of the holy father himself. We can indeed believe that the almighty power of God, which allowed the holy bishop Ambrose to attend the burial of the glorious St. Martin and to honor that holy prelate with his holy presence, also allowed his servant Francis to be present at the preaching of his true herald Anthony in order to attest to the truth of his words, especially those concerning Christ's cross, which Francis both carried and served.

When the Order was already widely spread and Francis was considering having the rule which had been approved by Innocent permanently confirmed by his successor Honorius, he was advised by the following revelation from God. It seemed to him that he had to gather some tiny bread crumbs from the ground and distribute them to many hungry friars who were standing around him. He was afraid to distribute such small crumbs lest they should fall from his hands. Then a voice spoke to him from above: "Francis, make one host out of all these crumbs and give it to those who want to eat it." When he did this, whoever did not receive it devoutly or despised the gift they had received suddenly appeared covered with leprosy. In the morning the holy man told all this to his companions, regretting that he did not understand the meaning of the vision. On the following day, while he was keeping watch in prayer, he heard a voice coming down from heaven, saying: "Francis the crumbs of last night are the words of the Gospel, the host is the rule and the leprosy is wickedness."

Since the profusion of texts from the Gospel had lengthened the rule unduly, Francis wished to condense it into a more concentrated form as the vision he was shown had commanded. Led by the Holy Spirit, he went up to a certain mountain with two of his companions where he fasted on bread and water and dictated the rule as the Holy Spirit suggested to him in prayer. When he came down from the mountain, he gave the rule to his vicar to keep. But after a few days had elapsed, the vicar claimed that he had lost it by an oversight. A second time the holy man went off to a place of solitude and at once rewrote the rule just as before, as if he were taking the words from the mouth of God. And he obtained confirmation for it, as he had desired, from the Lord Pope Honorius, in the eighth year of his pontificate.

> Fervently exhorting the friars
> to observe this rule,
> Francis used to say
> that nothing of what he had placed there
> came from his own efforts
> but that he dictated everything

just as it had been revealed by God.
To confirm this with greater certainty
by God's own testimony,
when only a few days had passed,
the stigmata of our Lord Jesus
were imprinted upon him
by the finger of the living God,
as the bull or seal
of Christ, the Supreme Pontiff,
for the complete confirmation of the rule
and approval of its author,
as will be described below,
after our exposition of his virtues.

Chapter 5

On the Austerity of His Life and How Creatures Provided Him Comfort

When Francis the man of God saw
that many were being inspired
by his example
to carry the cross of Christ with fervent spirit,
he himself like a good leader of Christ's army
was encouraged to reach the palm of victory
through the height of heroic virtue.
He directed his attention to this text of the
    Apostle:
"Those who belong to Christ
have crucified their flesh
with its passions and desires." (Gal. 5:24)

In order to carry in his own body the armor of the cross, he held in check his sensual appetites with such a rigid discipline that he scarcely took what was necessary for the sustenance of nature. He used to say that it would be difficult to satisfy the needs of the body without giving in to the earth-bound inclinations of the senses. Therefore when he was in good health, he scarcely ever allowed himself cooked food; and on the rare occasions when he did so, he either mixed it with ashes or made its flavor tasteless, usually by adding water. About his drinking wine, what shall I say since he would scarcely drink even enough water when he was burning with thirst? He discovered more effective methods of abstinence and daily improved in their exercise. Although he had already attained the height of perfection, he used to try new ways of punishing his sensual desires by afflicting his body, as if he were always beginning again.

When he went out among men, he conformed himself to his hosts in the food he ate because of the Gospel text (Luke 10:7). But when he returned home, he kept strictly his sparse and rigid abstinence. Thus he was austere toward himself but considerate toward his neighbor. Making himself obedient to the Gospel of Christ in everything, he gave an edifying example not only when he abstained but also when he ate. More often than not, the bare ground was a bed for his weary body; and he often used to sleep sitting up, with a piece of wood or a stone for a pillow. Clothed in a single poor little tunic, he served the Lord in cold and nakedness.

Once when he was asked how he could protect himself against the bite of the winter's frost with such thin clothing, he answered with a burning spirit: "If we were touched within by the flame of desire for our heavenly home, we would easily endure that exterior cold." In the matter of clothes, he had a horror for softness and loved coarseness, claiming that John the Baptist had been praised by the Lord for this (Matt. 11:8; Luke 7:25). If he felt the softness of a tunic that had been given to him, he used to sew pieces of cord on the inside because he used to say, according to the statement of Truth itself (Matt. 11:8), that we should look for soft clothes not in the huts of the poor but in the palaces of princes. For his own certain experience had taught him that demons were terrified by harshness but were inspired to tempt one more strongly by what is pleasant and soft.

One night, contrary to his custom, he had allowed a feather pillow to be placed under his head because of an illness in his head and eyes. The devil got into it, gave him no rest until morning and in many ways disturbed him from praying, until finally Francis called a companion and had him take the pillow with the devil in it far away out of his cell. But when the friar went out of the cell with the pillow, he lost the strength and use of his limbs, until at the sound of the holy father's voice, who was aware of this in spirit, his former strength of heart and body was fully restored to him.

He stood unbending in the discipline with which he watched over himself, and he took the greatest care to preserve purity of soul and body. Around the beginning of his conversion, in wintertime he often plunged into a ditch full of icy water in order to perfectly subjugate the enemy within and preserve the white robe of purity from the flames of sensual pleasure. He used to say that it should be incomparably more tolerable for a spiritual man to endure great cold in his flesh rather than to feel even slightly the heat of carnal lust in his heart.

One night when he was praying in his cell at the hermitage of Sarteano, the ancient enemy called him three times: "Francis, Francis, Francis!" When Francis replied and asked what he wanted, he continued deceitfully: "There is no sinner in the world whom God will not forgive if he is converted; but whoever kills himself by harsh penance will never find mercy for all eternity." At once the treachery of the enemy was revealed to the man of God: how the devil was trying to lead him back to lukewarmness. This was shown by what followed. For immediately after this, a temptation of the flesh seized him, inspired by the one "whose breath sets coals afire" (Job 41:21). When that lover of chastity felt it coming, he took off his clothes and began to lash himself very heavily with a cord, saying: "There, Brother Ass, this is how you ought to be treated, to bear the whip like this. The habit serves the religious state and presents a symbol of holiness. A lustful man has no right to steal it. If you want to go that way, then go!" Even more inspired by a wonderful fervor of spirit, he opened his cell and went out into the garden and plunged his poor naked body into the deep snow. Then with handfuls of snow he began to form seven snowmen, which he presented to himself, saying to his body: "Look, this larger one is your wife; those four are your two sons and two daughters; the other two are a servant and a maid whom you should have to serve you. Hurry, then, and clothe them since they are dying of cold. But if it is too much for you to care for so many, then take care to serve one Master!" At that the tempter went away conquered, and the holy man returned to his cell in victory. While he froze outwardly for penance's sake, he so quenched the fire of passion within that he hardly felt anything of that sort from that time on. A certain friar who was praying at the time saw in the bright moonlight everything that happened. When the man of God discovered that the friar had seen all of this that night, he gave him an account of the temptation and commanded him to tell no living person what he had seen as long as Francis himself lived.

He taught that not only the vices of the flesh should be mortified and fleshly impulses curbed but also that the exterior senses, through which death enters the soul, should be guarded with the greatest diligence. He solicitously commanded the friars to avoid familiarity with women, whether by sight or by conversation, which have often led many to a fall. He affirmed that through this sort of thing a weak spirit is often broken and a strong spirit weakened. He said that it is about as easy for one who has much contact with women—unless he be a man of the most proven virtue—to avoid contamination from them as "to walk in fire and not to burn one's feet" (Prov. 6:28). He himself so "turned aside his eyes lest they see vanity" of this kind (Ps. 119:37) that he scarcely recognized any woman by her face, as he once said to a companion. For he did not think it was safe to drink into one's interior such images of woman's form, which could rekindle the fire in an already tamed flesh or stain the brightness of a pure heart. He used to say that conversation with a woman was frivolous except only for confession or very brief instruction, according to what their salvation requires and respectability allows. "What business," he asked, "should a religious transact with a woman except when she makes a devout request for holy penance or for advice concerning a better life? Out of too much self-confidence one is less on guard against the enemy, and if the devil can claim as his own even one hair from a man, he will soon make it grow into a beam."

He taught the friars to flee with all their might from idleness, the cesspool of all evil thoughts; and he demonstrated to them by his own example that they should master their rebellious and lazy flesh by constant discipline and useful work. He used to call his body Brother Ass, for he felt it should be subjected to heavy labor, beaten frequently with whips and fed with the poorest food. If he saw that an idle and vagrant friar wanted to be fed by the labor of others, he thought he should be called Brother Fly, because he did nothing good himself but poisoned the good done by others and so rendered himself useless and obnoxious to all. On account of this he once said: "I want my friars to work and to be kept busy lest by giving themselves to idleness their hearts and tongues wander to unlawful things." He strongly wished that the friars observe the silence recommended by the Gospel, that is, to abstain carefully at all times from every idle word that they would have to render an account of on the day of judgment. But if he found a friar given to empty babbling, he used to reprimand him sharply, affirming that a modest silence is the guardian of a pure heart and no small virtue itself, in view of the fact that death and life are said to be in the power of the tongue (Prov. 18:21), not so much because of taste but because of speech.

Although he energetically urged the friars to lead an austere life, he was not pleased by an overstrict severity that did not put on a heart of compassion and was not seasoned with the salt of discretion. One night a friar was tormented with hunger because of his excessive fasting and was unable to get any rest. When the devoted shepherd realized that danger threatened one of his sheep, he called the friar and put some bread before him. Then, to take away his embarrassment, Francis himself began to eat first and affectionately invited him to eat. The friar overcame his embarrassment and took the food, overjoyed that through the discreet condescension of his shepherd he had avoided harm to his body and received an edifying example of no small proportion. When morning came, the man of God called the friars together and told them what had happened during the night, adding this advice: "Brothers, in this incident let the charity and not the food be an example to you." He taught them besides to follow prudence as the charioteer of the virtues, not the prudence which the flesh recommends, but the prudence taught by Christ, whose most holy life expressed for us the model of perfection.

> Encompassed by the weakness of the flesh,
> man cannot follow
> the spotless crucified Lamb so perfectly
> as to avoid contacting any filth.
> Therefore Francis taught
> that those who strive after the perfect life
> should cleanse themselves daily
> with streams of tears.
> Although he had already attained extraordinary
>   purity
> of heart and body,
> he did not cease to cleanse the eyes of his soul
> with a continuous flood of tears,

unconcerned about the loss of his bodily sight.
When he had incurred a very serious eye illness
from his continuous weeping,
and a doctor advised him to restrain his tears
if he wanted to avoid losing his sight,
the holy man answered:
"Brother doctor,
we should not stave off
a visitation of heavenly light even a little
because of love of the light,
which we have in common with flies.
For the body receives the gift of light
for the sake of the spirit
and not the spirit for the sake of the body."
He preferred to lose his sight
rather than to repress the devotion of his spirit
and hold back the tears
which cleansed his interior vision
so that he could see God.

Once he was advised by doctors and strongly urged by the friars
to allow himself to be cauterized. The man of God agreed humbly
because he realized that it would be at once good for his health
and harsh on his body. So a surgeon was called, and when he
came, he placed an iron in the fire for performing the cauteriza-
tion. But Christ's servant encouraged his body, which was now
struck with horror, and began to speak to the fire as a friend: "My
brother fire, whose beauty is the envy of all other creatures, the
Most High has created you strong, beautiful and useful. Be kind
to me in this hour, be courteous! I beseech the great Lord who

created you to temper your heat for me so that you will burn gently and I can endure it." When he had finished his prayer, he made the sign of the cross over the instrument that glowed with fire, and he waited unafraid. The iron was plunged hissing into the sensitive flesh and was drawn from his ear to his eyebrow in the process of cauterizing. How much pain the fire caused, the holy man himself expressed: "Praise the Most High," he said to the friars, "because I tell you truly, I felt neither the heat of the fire nor any pain in my flesh." And turning to the doctor, he said: "If my flesh is not well cauterized, then do it again!" The experienced doctor marveled at such strength of spirit in his weak body, and he proclaimed it a divine miracle, saying: "I say to you, brothers, I have seen wonderful things today."

> Francis had reached such purity
> that his body was in remarkable harmony
> with his spirit
> and his spirit with God.
> As a result God ordained
> that creation which serves its Maker
> should be subject in an extraordinary way
> to his will and command.

Another time when he was suffering from a very serious illness at the hermitage of Sant' Urbano, feeling his physical weakness, he asked for a drink of wine. He was told that there was no wine to give him; so he ordered water, and when it was brought, he blessed it with the sign of the cross. At once what had been pure water was changed into the best wine; and what the poverty of this deserted place could not provide was obtained by the purity of the holy man. With the taste of this wine, he immediately regained his health so easily that the newness of the taste and the recovery of his health, by supernaturally renewing the drink and the one who drank, confirmed by a double testimony that he had perfectly put off the old man and put on the new.

Not only did creation serve God's servant at his beck and call, but the Creator's providence itself everywhere inclined itself to his good pleasure. One time when his body was weighed down by many forms of illness, he had the desire to hear some music to awaken and delight his spirit. But since it was considered inappropriate that this should be done for him by human musicians, angels came to indulge the holy man's wish. One night when he was watching and meditating about the Lord, he suddenly heard the sound of a lute playing wonderful harmony and a very sweet melody. No one was seen, but he was aware that the musician was moving back and forth by the fluctuation of the sound. With his spirit directed to God, Francis enjoyed so thoroughly the beauty of that sweet-sounding song that he thought he had been transported to another world. This did not remain hidden from the friars who were close to him, for they often used to see clear indications that he was visited by the Lord, who gave him such overwhelming and frequent consolation that he could not hide it completely.

At another time when the man of God and a companion were walking on the banks of the Po while on a journey of preaching

between Lombardy and the Marches of Treviso, they were overtaken by the darkness of night. The road was exposed to many
great dangers because of the darkness, the river and some
swamps. His companion said to the holy man: "Pray, father, that
we may be saved from these threatening dangers!" Full of confidence, the man of God answered him: "God has the power, if it
pleases him in his sweetness, to disperse this darkness and give us
the benefit of light." Scarcely had he finished speaking when,
behold, such a great light began to shine around them with a
heavenly radiance that they could see in clear light not only the
road, but also many other things all around, although the night
remained dark elsewhere. By the guidance of this light they were
led physically and comforted spiritually; singing hymns of praise
to God they arrived safely at their lodging, which was quite a
stretch of road away.

> Consider carefully
> the marvelous purity and the degree of virtue
> that Francis attained.
> At his mere wish
> fire tempered its heat,
> water changed its taste,
> an angelic melody brought him comfort
> and a divine light gave him guidance.
> Thus it is proven
> that all of creation came to the service
> of the sanctified senses
> of this holy man.

Chapter 6

On His Humility and Obedience and God's Condescension to His Slightest Wish

Humility,
the guardian and the ornament
of all the virtues,
had filled the man of God in copious
    abundance.
In his own estimation
he was nothing but a sinner,
although in truth he was
a resplendent mirror
of all holiness.
He strove to build himself up
upon this virtue
like an architect laying the foundations,
for he had learned this
from Christ.
He used to say that it was for this reason
that the Son of God came down
from the height of his Father's bosom
to our lowly estate
so that our Lord and Teacher might teach
    humility
in both word and example.

Therefore as Christ's disciple,
he strove to appear worthless
in his own eyes and those of others,
recalling what had been said
by his supreme Teacher:
"What is highly esteemed among men
is an abomination before God" (Luke 16:15).
He often used to make this statement:
"What a man is in God's eyes,
that he is
and nothing more."
Therefore, judging that it was foolish
to be elated by worldly approval,
he rejoiced in insults
and was saddened by praise.
He preferred to hear himself
blamed rather than praised,
knowing that blame would lead him
to amend his life,
while praise would drive him to a fall.
And so when people extolled the merits
of his holiness,
he commanded one of the friars
to do the opposite
and to impress upon his ears
insulting words.
When that friar,
although unwilling, called him
boorish and mercenary, unskilled and useless,
he would reply
with inner joy shining on his face:

"May the Lord bless you,
my beloved son,
for it is you that speak the very truth
and what the son of Peter Bernardone should
    hear."

In order to render himself contemptible to others, he did not spare himself the embarrassment of bringing up his own faults when he preached before all the people. Once it happened that when he was weighed down with sickness, he relaxed a little the rigor of his abstinence in order to recover his health. When his strength of body returned, he was aroused to insult his own body out of true self-contempt: "It is not right," he said, "that the people should believe I am abstaining while, in fact, I eat meat on the sly." Inflamed with the spirit of true humility, he called the people together in the square of the town of Assisi and solemnly entered the principal church with many of the friars whom he had brought with him. With a rope tied around his neck and stripped to his underwear, he had himself dragged before the eyes of all to the stone where criminals received their punishment. He climbed up upon the stone and preached with much vigor and spirit although he was suffering from a fever and the weather was bitter cold. He asserted to all his hearers that he should not be honored as a spiritual man but rather he should be despised by all as a carnal man and a glutton. Therefore those who had gathered there were amazed at so great a spectacle. They were well aware of his austerity, and so their hearts were struck with compunction; but they professed his humility was easier to admire than to imitate.

Although this incident seemed to be more a portent like that of the Prophet (Isa. 20:3) than an example, nevertheless it was a lesson in true humility instructing the follower of Christ that he should despise the fame of transitory praise, suppress the arrogance of bloated bragging and reject the lies of deceptive pretense.

He often did many things like this so that outwardly he might become like a discarded utensil while inwardly possessing the spirit of holiness. He strove to hide the gifts of his Lord in the secret recesses of his heart, not wanting them to be exposed to praise, which could be an occasion of a fall. For often when he was praised by the crowds, he would answer like this: "I could still have sons and daughters; don't praise me as if I were secure! No one should be praised whose end is still uncertain." This is what he would say to those who praised him, and to himself he would say: "If the Most High had given so much to a brigand, he would be more grateful than you, Francis." He often used to tell the friars: "No one should flatter himself for doing anything a sinner can also do. A sinner," he said, "can fast, pray, weep and mortify his flesh. This one thing he cannot do: be faithful to his Lord. Therefore we should glory in this: if we give back to the Lord the glory that is his, if we serve him faithfully and ascribe to him whatever he gives to us."

In order to profit in many ways like the merchant in the Gospel and to use all the present time to gain merit, he wanted to be a subject rather than a superior, to obey rather than command. Therefore he relinquished his office as general and looked for a guardian whose will he would obey in all things. He used to say that the fruits of holy obedience are so abundant that for those who submit their necks to its yoke not an hour passes without making a profit. Therefore he used to always promise and observe obedience to whatever friar went with him on journeys. Once he said to his companions: "Among the many other things that the kindness of God has generously bestowed upon me, it has granted me this grace: that I would obey a novice of one hour, if he were given to me as my guardian, as diligently as I would obey the oldest and most discreet friar. A subject," he said, "should not consider the man in his superior but rather Christ, for whose love he is a subject. The more contemptible the superior, the more pleasing is the humility of the one who obeys."

On one occasion when he was asked who should be considered truly obedient, he gave as an example the comparison with a dead body. "Take a corpse," he said, "and put it where you will! You will see that it does not resist being moved, nor murmur about its position nor protest when it is cast aside. If it is placed on a throne, it will not raise its eyes up, but cast them down. If it is clothed in purple, it will look twice as pale. This," he said, "is a truly obedient man. He does not judge why he is moved; he does not care where he is placed; he does not insist on being transferred. If he is raised to an office, he retains his customary humility. The more he is honored, the more unworthy he considers himself."

Once he told his companion: "I would not seem to myself to be a Friar Minor unless I were in the state I will describe to you. Suppose, as superior of the friars, I go to the chapter, preach and admonish the friars and at the end they answer back: "You are not suitable for us because you are illiterate, without eloquence and an ignorant simpleton." Finally I am thrown out with reproaches and despised by all. I tell you that if I did not listen to these words with the same expression on my face, with the same joy and with the same determination for holiness, I am in no way a Friar Minor." And he added: "In the office of superior there is danger of a fall, in praise a precipice and in the humility of being a subject profit for the soul. Why, then, do we direct our attention to the dangers rather than to profit, when it is to gain profit that we have been given time?"

For this reason
Francis,
the model of humility,
wanted his friars to be called Minor
and the superiors of his Order to be called
    servants,
in order to use the very words of the Gospel
which he had promised to observe
and in order that his followers
might learn from this very name
that they had come to the school
of the humble Christ
to learn humility.
Jesus Christ,
the teacher of humility,
instructed his disciples in true humility
by saying: "Whoever wishes to become great
    among you,

> let him be your servant;
> and whoever wishes to be first among you
> will be your slave." (Matt. 20:26–27)

When the cardinal of Ostia, the chief protector and promoter of the Order of Friars Minor (who afterwards, as the holy man had prophesied, was elevated to the honor of the supreme pontificate and was called Gregory IX) asked him whether he would allow his friars to be promoted to ecclesiastical offices, he responded: "Lord, my brothers are called Minors so that they will not presume to become great men. If you want them to bear fruit in the Church of God, hold them and preserve them in the state to which they have been called, and by no means permit them to rise to ecclesiastical offices."

Because he preferred humility to honors both in himself and in all his subjects, God, the lover of the humble, judged him worthy of the highest honors. This was shown in a vision from heaven to one of the friars, a man of outstanding virtue and devotion. When he was in the company of the man of God and was praying fervently with him in a deserted church, he was rapt in ecstasy and saw among the many thrones in heaven one more honorable than the rest, ornamented with precious stones and shining with the fullness of glory. He marveled within himself at the splendor of this lofty throne and began to wonder anxiously who would be raised to it. In the midst of these thoughts he heard a voice saying to him: "This throne belonged to one of the fallen angels and now is reserved for the humble Francis." At length, when the friar came back to himself from his ecstasy, he followed the blessed man as usual when he left the church. As they went along the road talking together about God, the friar, not unmindful of his vision, skillfully asked Francis what he thought of himself. The humble servant of Christ said to him: "I see myself as the greatest of sinners." When the friar said to the contrary that he could not say or feel that with a good conscience, Francis continued: "If Christ had shown as much mercy to the greatest criminal, I am convinced that he would be much more grateful to God than I." At hearing such remarkable humility, the friar was convinced of the truth of his vision, knowing from the testimony of the Gospel (Matt. 23:12; Luke 1:52) that the truly humble will be exalted to the height of glory from which the proud have been cast out.

Another time, when he was praying in an abandoned church at Monte Casale in the province of Massa, he learned through the spirit that sacred relics had been left there. When he sadly reflected that they had been for a long time deprived of the honor due to them, he ordered the friars to bring them with reverence to their place. But when Francis for some reason had gone away, his sons forgot about his command and neglected the merit of obedience. One day when they wanted to celebrate the sacred mysteries and removed the cover from the altar, they were astonished to find some very beautiful and fragrant bones. What they were looking upon were the relics, which had been brought there by God's power, not by human hands. When the man devoted to God returned a little later, he began to diligently inquire if what he had ordered about the relics had been carried out. Humbly confessing the guilt of their neglected obedience, the friars merited pardon along with a penance. And the holy man said: "Blessed be my Lord and God who carried out himself what you should have done."

> Consider diligently
> the care of divine providence for our dust,
> and the excellence of the virtue
> of the humble Francis
> in the eyes of God.
> For when men neglected his commands,
> God himself
> obeyed his wishes.

One time when he came to Imola, he went to the bishop of the town and humbly asked his permission to call the people together and preach to them. The bishop replied harshly: "My preaching should be quite enough for them, brother." This truly humble man bowed his head and went away, but in less than an hour he came back. The bishop was annoyed and asked him what he was looking for a second time. Then Francis replied with a humble heart and a humble tone of voice: "My lord, if a father throws his son out one door, he has to come in another." Conquered by this humility, the bishop embraced him enthusiastically and said: "From now on you and all your friars may preach in my diocese with my general permission, because your holy humility has won this."

It happened once that he came to Arezzo at a time when the whole city was shaken by civil war and was on the brink of destruction. Given hospitality in the outskirts, he saw over the city devils rejoicing and inflaming the troubled citizens to mutual slaughter. In order to put to flight those seditious spiritual powers, he sent Brother Silvester, a man of dovelike simplicity, before him like a herald, saying: "Go before the gate of the city and on the part of Almighty God command the devils to leave immediately!" This truly obedient man hastened to carry out his father's orders, and singing psalms of praise before the face of the Lord, he began to shout out forcefully before the gate of the city: "On the part of Almighty God and at the command of his servant Francis, depart far from here, all you devils." At once the city returned to peace and all the citizens reformed their civil statutes very peacefully. Once the raging pride of the devils, which had surrounded the city like a siege, had been driven out, the wisdom of a poor man, namely the humility of Francis, entered in, brought back peace and saved the city. By his lofty virtue of humble obedience, he had gained such powerful control over those rebellious and obstinate spirits that he could repress their ferocious brashness and drive back their savage violence.

The proud demons flee from the lofty virtues of the humble unless occasionally the divine goodness should permit the demons to buffet them in order to protect their humility, as the Apostle Paul writes about himself (2 Cor. 12:7) and Francis learned through his own experience. Once he had been asked by Lord Leo, cardinal of the church of the Holy Cross, to stay for a little while with him in Rome, and he humbly accepted out of respect and affection. The first night he spent there, when he wanted to rest after his prayer, the devils came upon the soldier of

Christ and attacked him fiercely. They beat him severely for a long time and in the end left him half dead. As they departed, the man of God called his companion and, when he came, told him what had happened, adding: "Brother, I believe that the devils can do nothing that God's providence does not allow. Therefore they attacked me so fiercely now because my staying in the court of great personages does not present a good example. My friars who live in poor places, hearing that I am staying with cardinals, will perhaps suspect that I am involved in worldly affairs, puffed up by honors and wallowing in pleasure. Therefore I judge that it is better for one who is set as an example to avoid courts and to live humbly among the humble in humble places, in order to strengthen those who are bearing severe poverty by bearing the same himself." In the morning, then, they went to the cardinal, excused themselves humbly and said good-bye.

The holy man abhorred pride, the source of all evil, and dis-obedience, its worst offspring, but he welcomed the humility of repentance with no less intensity. It happened once that a friar who had done something against the law of obedience was brought to him to be punished according to justice. Seeing that the friar showed clear signs of being truly sorry, the man of God was drawn to be easy on him out of love of humility. However, lest this easy forgiveness be an incentive for others to fail in their duty, he ordered that the friar's hood be taken off and thrown into the fire so that all could see what and how harsh a punish-ment the offense of disobedience deserved. When the hood had been within the fire for a while, he ordered that it be taken out of the flames and returned to the humbly repentant friar. What a marvel! The hood was taken out of the middle of the flames, but showed no trace of a burn. Thus with this one miracle God showed his approval both of the holy man's virtue and of the humility of repentance.

> Francis's humility, therefore,
> is worthy of imitation.
> It merited such marvelous honor
> even on earth
> that it inclined God to his wishes
> and changed the attitude of men,
> repulsed the obstinacy of demons
> at his command,
> and held in check voracious flames
> at his mere nod.
> Truly this is the humility
> which exalts those who possess it,
> while it shows reverence to all
> and deserves honor from all.

Chapter 7

On His Love of Poverty and the Miraculous Fulfillment of His Needs

Among the gifts of grace
which Francis received
from God the generous Giver,
he merited
as a special privilege
to grow in the riches of simplicity
through his love
of the highest poverty.
The holy man saw
that poverty was the close companion
of the Son of God,
and now that it was rejected by the whole
    world,
he was eager to espouse it
in everlasting love.
For the sake of poverty
he not only left his father and mother,
but also gave away
everything he had.
No one was so greedy for gold
as he was for poverty;
nor was anyone so anxious

to guard his treasure
as he was in guarding
this pearl of the Gospel.
In this especially would his sight be offended
if he saw in the friars
anything which did not accord completely
with poverty.
Indeed, from the beginning of his religious life
until his death,
his only riches were
a tunic, a cord and underclothes;
and with this much
he was content.
He used to frequently call to mind with tears
the poverty of Jesus Christ and his mother,
claiming that it was
the queen of the virtues
because it shone forth so preeminently
in the King of Kings and in the Queen, his
mother.

When the friars asked him at a gathering what virtue does more to make one a friend of Christ, he replied as if opening up the hidden depths of his heart: "Know, brothers, that poverty is the special way to salvation, as the stimulus of humility and the root of perfection, whose fruit is manifold but hidden. This is the Gospel's treasure 'hidden in a field' (Matt. 13:44); to buy this we should sell everything, and in comparison to this we should spurn everything we cannot sell.

"Whoever desires to attain the height of poverty should

renounce in some way not only worldly wisdom but also learning, that having renounced such a possession, he might enter into the mighty works of the Lord and offer himself naked to the arms of the Crucified. No one can be said to have perfectly renounced the world if he still keeps the purse of his own opinion in the hidden recesses of his heart."

When speaking about poverty, he often proposed to the friars this text of the Gospel: "The foxes have their holes and the birds of the air their nests, but the Son of Man has nowhere to lay his head" (Matt. 8:20; Luke 9:58). For this reason he instructed the friars to build poor houses like those of the poor and to live in these not as their own, but like pilgrims and strangers in the house of another. For he used to say that the law of pilgrims was to take shelter under another's roof, to thirst for their homeland and to travel peacefully. Sometimes he ordered the friars to tear down a house they had built or to move out of it if he noticed something contrary to Gospel poverty either because they had appropriated it as their possession or because it was too sumptuous. He used to say that poverty was the foundation of the Order, on which the entire structure of their religious life so basically depended that it would stand firm if poverty were firm and collapse completely if poverty were undermined.

He taught, as he had learned from a revelation, that one entering the holy Order should begin from this text of the Gospel: "If you wish to be perfect, go, sell all that you have, and give to the poor" (Matt. 19:21). Only those who had given away all possessions and retained absolutely nothing did he admit to the Order, both on account of the text of the Gospel and lest scandal should arise over any possessions kept back. Thus when a man asked to be received into the Order in the Marches of Ancona, the true patriarch of the poor replied: "If you want to join Christ's poor, distribute what you have to the poor of the world." When he heard this, the man went off and, led by a carnal love, left his goods to his relatives, giving nothing to the poor. When the holy man heard him tell of this, he reproached him harshly and said: "Go on your way, Brother Fly, because you have not yet left your home and your kindred. You gave your goods to your relatives and you have cheated the poor; you are not worthy of the holy poor. You have begun with the flesh; you have laid a ruinous foundation for a spiritual structure." That carnal man returned to his relatives and reclaimed his goods, which he did not want to give to the poor, and so very quickly abandoned his virtuous intention.

Another time there was such a lack of resources at St. Mary of the Portiuncula that it was impossible to provide for the needs of the friars who were visiting there. Francis's vicar came to him, pointed out the destitution of the friars and asked permission to keep aside some of the goods of the novices when they entered so that the friars could have something to fall back on in case of necessity. Not without heavenly guidance, Francis said to him: "Let it be far from us, dearest brother, to sin against the rule for the sake of any man. I prefer that you strip the altar of the glorious Virgin, when necessity requires it, than to tamper even a little with the vow of poverty and the observance of the Gospel. The

Blessed Virgin will be more pleased to have her altar stripped and the Gospel counsel observed perfectly rather than to have her altar adorned and her Son's counsel neglected when we have promised to keep it."

One time when the man of God was going through Apulia near Bari with a companion, he found on the road a large purse, of the type they call *funda*, apparently bursting with money. His companion advised him and nagged him to pick up the purse from the ground and give the money to the poor. The man of God refused, claiming there was a trick of the devil in this purse they had found and that the friar was recommending something sinful rather than meritorious, namely to take what belonged to another and give it away. They left the place and hurried to finish the journey they had begun. But the friar was not yet satisfied, deluded as he was by a false sense of charity; he kept bothering the man of God as if the latter had no concern to relieve the destitution of the poor. Finally the patient man agreed to return to the place—not to carry out the friar's wish, but to uncover the devil's trickery. So he returned to the purse with the friar and with a young man who was on the road. After praying, he commanded his companion to pick it up. The friar was dumbfounded and trembled, for now he had a premonition of some diabolic manifestation. Nevertheless, because of the command of holy obedience, he drove away the doubt in his heart and stretched out his hand toward the purse; and behold, a large snake jumped out of the purse and suddenly disappeared along with it, showing the friar that this was the deception of the devil. The enemy's trickery and cunning were grasped, and the holy man said to his companion: "To the servants of God, brother, money is the very devil and a poisonous snake."

After this a remarkable thing happened to the holy man when he was going to the city of Siena on some necessary business. In a great plain between Campiglia and San Quirico he was met by three poor women who were exactly alike in height, age and appearance. They offered him the gift of a new salutation, saying: "Welcome, Lady Poverty!" When he heard this, the true lover of poverty was filled with unspeakable joy because there was nothing in him that he would rather have people acknowledge than what these women singled out.

> They suddenly disappeared,
> and when his companions considered
> their remarkable similarity,
> their novel greeting,
> their strange meeting and disappearance,
> they concluded
> not without reason
> that this had some mystical meaning
> for the holy man.
> It seemed that these three poor women
> who were so alike in appearance,
> who gave such an unusual greeting
> and disappeared so suddenly,
> appropriately showed that the beauty of Gospel
>   perfection,
> in poverty, chastity and obedience,

shone forth all perfectly equal
in the man of God
although he had chosen to glory above all
in the privilege of poverty
which he used to call
his mother, his bride and his lady.
It was in poverty that he desired
to surpass others
because from it he had learned
to regard himself
inferior to all.

Therefore whenever he saw anyone more poorly dressed than he, Francis immediately censured himself and roused himself to imitate him, as if he were competing in a rivalry over poverty and feared to be beaten by another. It once happened that he met a poor man on the road, and when he saw how ragged he was, his heart was struck, and he said to his companion sorrowfully: "This man's need puts us to shame, because we have chosen poverty as our wealth; and see, it shines more clearly in him."

For love of holy poverty, God's servant more gladly used the alms that had been begged from door to door than those that had been spontaneously offered. If he were invited by distinguished personages and they served a better table than usual in his honor, he would first beg some pieces of bread from the neighboring houses and then sit down at table, thus enriched by his poverty. He did this once when he had been invited by the lord bishop of Ostia, who held Christ's poor man in special affection. The bishop complained that Francis had disparaged the honor shown him by going out after alms when he was to share his hospitality at table. God's servant replied: "My lord, I have shown you great honor in honoring a greater Lord. For the Lord is pleased with poverty and especially with that poverty which involves voluntary begging for Christ. This is the royal dignity which the Lord Jesus assumed when he became poor for us that he might enrich us by his poverty and establish us as heirs and kings of the kingdom of heaven if we are truly poor in spirit. I do not wish to relinquish this royal dignity for a fief of false riches loaned to you for only an hour."

Sometimes he would exhort the friars to beg for alms with words such as these: "Go forth because in this last hour the Friars Minor have been given to the world that through them the elect might have the opportunity to fulfill what will be commended by the Judge as they hear those most sweet words: 'As long as you have done it to one of these, the least of my brothers, you did it to me'" (Matt. 25:40). Therefore he used to say that it was a delight to beg with the title of Friars Minor, which the Teacher of Gospel truth had so clearly expressed by his own mouth when rewarding the just. When there was an opportunity, he used to go begging on the principal feasts, saying that the prophecy "Man will eat the bread of Angels" (Ps. 78:25) is fulfilled in the holy poor. For he said that it is indeed the bread of angels that has been begged for the love of God and has been given for his love at the inspiration of the angels and gathered from door to door by holy poverty.

Once on an Easter Sunday he was staying at a hermitage that was so far from any houses that he could not conveniently go begging. And so in remembrance of him who appeared that very day in the guise of a pilgrim to his disciples on the road to Emmaus, Francis then begged alms from the friars themselves, like a pilgrim and beggar. When he had received it humbly, he informed them with holy eloquence that they should pass through the desert of the world like pilgrims and strangers and like true Hebrews continually celebrate in poverty of spirit the Lord's Pasch, that is his passing over from this world to the Father.

> Since, when he begged alms,
> he was motivated
> not by greed for profit but by liberty of spirit,
> God the Father of the poor
> seemed to have special care for him.

Once when this servant of the Lord was very ill at Nocera, he was brought back to Assisi by a formal embassy sent for that purpose out of devotion by the townspeople. While they were taking Christ's servant back, they came to a poor little village by the name of Satriano. Since their hunger and the hour called for food, they went out; but, finding nothing for sale, they returned empty-handed. The holy man told them: "You found nothing because you trust more in your flies than in God" (for he called coins flies). "Go back," he said, "to the houses which you have visited and humbly ask for an alms, offering God's love in place of money. Do not consider this shameful or cheap out of false esteem, because after man's sin that great Almsgiver has bestowed all things as alms to both the worthy and the unworthy, out of his abundant kindness." The knights put aside their embarrassment, readily begged for alms and bought more with the love of God than with money. Their hearts struck with compunction by God, the poor villagers generously gave not only what they had but also themselves. And so it happened that Francis's wealthy poverty supplied the need which money could not alleviate.

At the time when he was lying ill in a hermitage near Rieti, a doctor visited him often to care for him. Since the poor man of Christ was unable to pay him adequately for his services, the most generous God made up for the poor man and repaid the doctor for his devoted care with the following favor, so that he would not go without payment in the present life. The doctor's new house, which he had just spent all his money building, was threatened with collapse because of a wide crack in the wall, which reached from the top to the bottom—a collapse which seemed unavoidable by human means. Fully trusting in the merits of the holy man and out of the devotion of his great faith, he asked Francis's companions to give him something which the man of God had touched with his hands. After many requests he obtained a small amount of his hair, which he placed one evening in the crack in the wall. When he rose in the morning, he found that the crack had been so firmly closed that he could not pull out the hairs he had placed there nor could he find any trace of the crack. And so it happened that because he had dutifully ministered to the body of God's servant in its state of collapse, he avoided the danger of the collapse of his house.

Another time the man of God wanted to go to a hermitage where he could spend more time in contemplation. Because he was weak, he rode on an ass that belonged to a certain poor man. Since it was summertime and the man had to climb up the mountain following after God's servant, he became fatigued by the long and grueling journey. Weakened by a burning thirst, he began to cry out urgently to the saint: "Look, I'll die of thirst if I don't get a drink immediately." Without delay the man of God jumped off the ass, knelt on the ground, stretched forth his hands to heaven and did not cease praying until he knew that he had been heard. Finally, when he finished his prayer, he told the man: "Hurry to that rock and you will find running water which this very hour Christ has mercifully drawn out of the rock for you to drink." How amazing is God's condescension, which bows so easily to his servants! A thirsty man drank water from the rock by the power of another's prayer and took a drink from the solid stone. There was no stream of water there before, nor could any be found since, although a careful search was made.

How Christ multiplied food at sea through the merits of his poor man will be noted below. Here let it suffice to mention that with only a small amount of food which he had been given as alms, he saved the sailors from the danger of starvation and death for a number of days. From this one could clearly see that just as the servant of Almighty God was like Moses in drawing "water

from the rock" (Ps. 78:16; Exod. 17:1–7), so he was like Elisha in
the multiplication of provisions (2 Kings 4:1–8).

> Therefore, let all distrust be far
> from Christ's poor.
> For if Francis's poverty was so abundantly
>   sufficient
> that it supplied by miraculous power
> the needs of those who came to his aid,
> providing food, drink and housing
> when money, skill and natural means were
>   lacking,
> how much more will it merit
> those things that are given to all
> in the usual plan of divine providence.
> If a dry rock gave drink abundantly
> to a poor man who was thirsty
> at the word of another poor man,
> nothing at all
> will refuse its service
> to those who have left all
> for the Maker of all.

Chapter 8

On His Affectionate Piety and How Irrational Creatures Were Affectionate toward Him

True piety,
which according to the Apostle
is helpful for all things,
had so filled Francis's heart
and penetrated its depths
that it seemed to have appropriated the man
   of God
completely into its dominion.
This is what
drew him up to God
through devotion,
transformed him into Christ
through compassion,
attracted him to his neighbor
through condescension
and symbolically showed a return
to the state of original innocence
through universal reconciliation
with each and every thing.
Through this virtue
he was attracted to all things
in spiritual love,

especially to souls redeemed by the precious
  blood
of Jesus Christ.
When he saw them being stained
by the filth of sin,
he grieved with such tender pity
that he seemed like a mother
who was daily in labor pains
bringing them to birth in Christ.
This was his principal reason
for reverencing the ministers
of the word of God,
because with their devoted concern
for the conversion of sinners
they raise up seed for their dead brother,
namely Christ, crucified for us,
and guide them
with their concerned devotion.
He firmly held
that such work of mercy
was more acceptable
to the Father of mercies
than any sacrifice,
especially if this eagerness arose
out of perfect charity
more by example than by word,
more by tear-filled prayer
than by long-winded sermons.

He used to say that we should feel sorry for a preacher, as for a
man without real piety, who in his preaching does not seek the

salvation of souls but his own praise or who destroys with the evil of his life what he builds up with the truth of his teaching. He said that a simple tongue-tied friar should be preferred to such a preacher because he called others to good by his good example. And so he explained the text "So that the barren has borne many" (1 Samuel 2:5) as follows: "The barren woman," he said, "is that poor little friar who does not have the duty of bringing forth children in the Church. He will bring forth many at the judgment because those he is now converting to Christ by his private prayers, the Judge will ascribe to his glory. The continuation of the text, "she that has many children will be weakened," means that a vain and loquacious preacher who now rejoices over the many as if he had brought them forth by his own power will then realize that he had nothing of his own involved with them."

He longed with heartfelt piety and burned with ardent zeal for the salvation of souls. He used to say that he was filled with the sweetest fragrance and anointed with precious ointment when he heard that many were being converted to the way of truth by the fragrant reputation of the holy friars in the distant regions of the world. When he heard of such things, he rejoiced in spirit and heaped his most desirable blessings upon those friars who by word or deed led sinners to the love of Christ. Thus also the ones who dishonored the religious life by their evil deeds incurred his severest curse: "May you, most holy Lord, and the whole celestial court, and I too, your little one, curse them who disrupt and destroy by their bad example what you have built up and do not cease to build up through the holy friars of this Order." He was often so deeply saddened by scandal given to the weak that he felt he would be overcome unless he had been supported by God's merciful consolation. Once when he was disturbed by certain instances of bad example and anxiously prayed to the merciful Father for his sons, he received this response from the Lord: "What's all this worry, you poor bit of a man? Did I so make you the shepherd of my Order that you can forget that it is I who am its principal protector? I chose you for this because you are a simple man and what I would do in you would be ascribed to divine grace and not to human effort. I have called the friars, I will preserve and feed them; and if some fall away, I will call others—indeed, even if they are yet unborn, I will have them born. No matter how severely this poor little Order is shaken, it will always remain safe by my grace."

He abhorred like a snakebite the vice of detraction, as a foe to the source of piety and grace; and he firmly held it to be a devastating plague and an abomination to God's mercy because the detractor feeds on the blood of the souls which he kills with the sword of his tongue. Once when he heard a friar blacken the reputation of another, he turned to his vicar and said: "Arise, arise, examine diligently and if you find that the friar accused is innocent, make an example of the accuser by correcting him severely." Sometimes he decreed that a friar who had stripped another friar of his good name should be stripped of his habit and that he should not be allowed to raise his eyes to God until he first did his best to restore what he had taken away. He used to say that the impiety of detractors is a much greater sin than that of robbers; for the law of Christ, which is fulfilled in the observance of piety, obliges us to desire the well-being of the soul more than the body.

He responded with a remarkably tender compassion to those suffering from any bodily affliction. If he saw signs of poverty in anyone or signs of deprivation, he referred them to Christ in the sweetness of his pious heart. He had an inborn kindness which was doubled by the kindness of Christ infused in him from above. Therefore his soul melted at the sight of the poor and infirm, and to those to whom he could not extend a helping hand he extended his affection. Once it happened that one of the friars responded gruffly to a beggar who had asked for an alms at an inconvenient time. When the devoted lover of the poor heard this, he ordered the friar to strip himself, cast himself at the beggar's feet, confess his guilt and beg for his prayers and forgiveness. When he had done this humbly, the father added sweetly: "When you see a poor man, my brother, an image of the Lord and his poor mother is being placed before you. Likewise in the case of the sick, consider the physical weakness which the Lord took upon himself." That most Christian pauper saw Christ's image in all the poor; and when he met them, he not only generously gave them even the necessities of life that had been given to him, but he believed that these should be given them as if theirs by right. It happened once that a poor man met him on his return from Siena, when because of an illness he was wearing a short mantle over his habit. When his kind eye observed the man's misery, he said to his companion: "We should return this mantle to this poor man because it is his. For we got it on loan until we should find someone poorer than ourselves." But his companion, considering the need of his devoted father, obstinately refused, lest Francis provide for another by neglecting himself. But Francis said: "I believe that the great Almsgiver will charge me with theft if I do not give what I have to one who needs it more." Therefore concerning all that was given him to relieve the needs of his body, he was accustomed to ask the permission of the donors to give it away if he should meet someone in greater need. He spared nothing at all, neither mantles, tunics nor books; not even decorations from the altar—all these he gave to the poor when he could, in order to fulfill his obligation of piety. When he met the poor along the road carrying heavy burdens, he often took the load on his own weak shoulders.

When he considered the primordial source of all things, he was filled with even more abundant piety, calling creatures, no matter how small, by the name of brother or sister, because he knew they had the same source as himself. However, he embraced more affectionately and sweetly those creatures which present a natural reflection of Christ's merciful gentleness and represent him in Scriptural symbolism. He often paid to ransom lambs that were being led to their death, remembering that most gentle Lamb who willed to be led to slaughter to pay the ransom of sinners.

One time when God's servant was lodging at the monastery of San Verecondo in the diocese of Gubbio, a sheep gave birth to a little lamb during the night. There was a ferocious sow there, which did not spare the life of the innocent lamb, but killed it with her ravenous bite. When he heard of this, the devoted father

was moved by wonderful compassion and, remembering the
Lamb without stain, grieved in the presence of all over the death
of the little lamb, saying: "Alas, brother lamb, innocent animal,
you represent Christ to men. A curse on that impious beast that
killed you; may no man or beast ever eat of her." Remarkably, the
evil sow immediately became ill and after paying for her deed
with three days of bodily punishment she finally suffered aveng-
ing death. She was thrown into the monastery ditch and lay there
for a long time dried up like a board, and did not serve as food
for any hungry animal.

> Let the impiety of men, therefore,
> be warned
> how great a punishment will be inflicted on it
> at the end of time,
> if the cruelty of an animal
> was punished
> with so horrible a death.
> Let also the devotion of the faithful consider
> that the marvelous power and abundant
> sweetness
> of the piety of God's servant
> was so great
> that it was acknowledged in their own way
> even by animals.

When Francis was traveling near the city of Siena, he came upon
a large flock of sheep in a pasture. When he greeted them kindly,
as he was accustomed to do, they all stopped grazing and ran to

him, lifting their heads and fixing their eyes on him. They gave him such a welcome that the shepherds and the friars were amazed to see the lambs and even the rams frisking about him in such an extraordinary way.

Another time at St. Mary of the Portiuncula the man of God was offered a sheep, which he gratefully accepted in his love of that innocence and simplicity which the sheep by its nature reflects. The pious man admonished the little sheep to praise God attentively and to avoid giving any offense to the friars. The sheep carefully observed his instructions, as if it recognized the piety of the man of God. For when it heard the friars chanting in choir, it would enter the church, genuflect without instructions from anyone, and bleat before the altar of the Virgin, the mother of the Lamb, as if it wished to greet her. Besides, when the most sacred body of Christ was elevated at mass, it would bow down on bended knees as if this reverent animal were reproaching those who were not devout and inviting the devout to reverence the sacrament.

Once in Rome he had with him a little lamb out of reverence for the most gentle Lamb of God. At his departure he left it in the care of the noble matron, the Lady Jacoba of Settesoli. Now the lamb went with the lady to church, standing reverently by her side as her inseparable companion, as if it had been trained in spiritual matters by the saint. If the lady was late in rising in the morning, the lamb rose and nudged her with its horns and woke her with its bleating, urging her with its nods and gestures to hurry to the church. On account of this, the lamb, which was

Francis's disciple and had now become a master of devotion, was held by the lady as an object of wonder and love.

Another time at Greccio a live hare was offered to the man of God, which he placed on the ground and let it free to go where it wished. But when the kind father called, it ran and jumped into his arms. He fondled it with warm affection and seemed to pity it like a mother. After warning it gently not to let itself be caught again, he let it go free. But as often as he placed it on the ground to run away, it always came back to the father's arms, as if in some secret way it perceived the kind feeling he had for it. Finally, at the father's command, the friars carried it away to a safer place far from the haunts of men.

In the same way on an island in the lake of Perugia a rabbit was caught and offered to the man of God. Although it fled from everyone else, it entrusted itself to his hands and his heart as if to the security of its home. When he was hurrying across the Lake of Rieti to the hermitage of Greccio, out of devotion a fisherman offered him a waterfowl. He took it gladly and opened his hands to let it go, but it did not want to. He prayed for a long time with his eyes turned to heaven. After more than an hour, he came back to himself as if from another realm and gently told the bird again to go away and praise God. Having received his permission with a blessing, the bird expressed its joy in the movements of its body, and flew away. On the same lake in a similar way he was offered a large live fish, which he addressed as brother in his usual way and put back into the water by the boat. The fish played about in the water in front of the man of God; and as if it were attracted by his love, it would not go away from the ship until it received from him his permission with a blessing.

Another time when he was walking with a friar through the marshes of Venice, he came upon a large flock of birds singing among the reeds. When he saw them, he said to his companion: "Our sisters the birds are praising their Creator; so we should go in among them and chant the Lord's praises and the canonical hours." When they had entered among them, the birds did not move from the place; and on account of the noise the birds were making, they could not hear each other saying the hours. The saint turned to the birds and said: "Sister birds, stop singing until we have done our duty of praising God!" At once they were silent and remained in silence as long as it took the friars to say the hours at length and to finish their praises. Then the holy man of God gave them permission to sing again. When the man of God gave them permission, they immediately resumed singing in their usual way.

A cricket used to perch on a fig tree beside the cell of the man of God at St. Mary of the Portiuncula and sing, arousing with its songs the Lord's servant to sing more frequently the divine praises, for he had learned to marvel at the Creator's magnificence even in insignificant creatures. He called it one day, and it flew upon his hand as if it had been taught by God. He said to it: "Sing, my sister cricket, praise the Lord Creator with your joyful song!" It obeyed without delay and began to sing; nor did it stop until at his command it flew back to its usual place. There it remained for eight days, coming each day, singing and returning, all at his command. Finally the man of God said to his companions: "Let us give our sister cricket permission to go away now, for she has cheered us enough with her singing and has aroused us to praise God over the space of eight days." With his permission, it departed and never appeared there again, as if it did not dare to disobey his command in the slightest way.

When he was ill at Siena, a nobleman sent him a live pheasant he had recently caught. The moment it saw and heard the holy man, it was drawn to him with such affection that it would in no way allow itself to be separated from him. Many times it was placed outside the friars' place in the vineyard so that it could go away if it wanted. But every time it ran right back to the father as if it had always been reared by him. Then it was given to a man who used to visit God's servant out of devotion, but it absolutely refused to eat, as if it were upset at being out of the sight of the devoted father. It was finally brought back to God's servant and, as soon as it saw him, showed signs of joy and ate heartily.

When he went to the hermitage of La Verna to observe a forty-day fast in honor of the Archangel Michael, birds of different kinds flew around his cell, with melodious singing and joyful movements, as if rejoicing at his arrival, and seemed to be inviting and enticing the devoted father to stay. When he saw this, he said to his companion: "I see, brother, that it is God's will that we stay here for some time, for our sisters the birds seem so delighted at our presence." When he extended his stay there, a falcon that had built its nest there became deeply attached to him as a friend. For at the hour of the night when the holy man used to rise for the divine office, the falcon always came to wake him by making noise and singing. This pleased God's servant very much because the falcon was so solicitous toward him that it shook out of him all sluggish laziness. But when Christ's servant was more than usually weighed down with illness, the falcon had pity and did not impose such early vigils on him. As if instructed by God, about dawn it would ring the bell of its voice with a light touch.

> There certainly seems to have been
> a divine prophecy
> both in the joy of the different kinds of birds
> and in the song of the falcon—
> a prophecy
> of the time when
> this praiser and worshiper of God
> would be lifted up
> on the wings of contemplation
> and there would be exalted
> with a Seraphic vision.

Once when he was staying in the hermitage at Greccio, the local inhabitants were being troubled by many evils. For a pack of ravenous wolves were devouring not only animals but even men, and every year hail storms were devastating the fields and vineyards. When the herald of the holy Gospel preached to these people who were thus afflicted, he said to them: "For the honor and praise of Almighty God I promise you that all this pestilence will depart and the Lord will look kindly upon you and give you an increase of temporal goods if you believe me and show mercy to

yourselves by making a good confession and 'bring forth fruits
worthy of repentance' (Matt. 3:8). Again I announce to you that
if you are ungrateful for his gifts and 'return to your vomit' (Prov.
26:11), the plague will be renewed, punishment will be doubled
and even greater wrath will rage against you." The people did
penance at his exhortation, and from that hour, the damage
ceased, the dangers passed and neither the wolves nor the hail
caused any further trouble. Furthermore, what is even greater, if
hail came over the fields of their neighbors and approached their
borders, it either stopped there or was diverted to another area.

> The hail kept the pact
> of God's servant
> and so too did the wolves;
> nor did they try to rage anymore
> contrary to the law of piety
> against men who had been converted to piety,
> as long as, according to their agreement,
> the people did not act impiously
> against God's most pious laws.
> Therefore, we should respond piously
> to the piety
> of this blessed man,
> which had such remarkable
> sweetness and power
> that it subdued ferocious beasts,
> tamed the wild,
> trained the tame
> and bent to his obedience
> the brute beasts that had rebelled

against fallen mankind.
Truly this is the virtue
that unites all creatures in brotherhood
and is helpful for all things
since it has the promise of the present life,
and of the life to come.

Chapter 9

On the Fervor of His Charity and His Desire for Martyrdom

Who can describe
the fervent charity
which burned within Francis, the friend of the
    Bridegroom?
Like a glowing coal,
he seemed totally absorbed
in the flame of divine love.
Whenever he heard of the love of God,
he was at once excited, moved and inflamed
as if an inner chord of his heart
had been plucked by the plectrum
of the external voice.
He used to say
that to offer the love of God in exchange for
    an alms
was a noble prodigality
and that those who valued it less than money
were most foolish,
because the incalculable price of divine love
    alone
was sufficient to purchase
the kingdom of heaven.
And he used to say

that greatly should the love be loved
of him who loved us so greatly.
Aroused by all things to the love of God,
he rejoiced in all the works of the Lord's hands
and from these joy-producing manifestations
he rose to their life-giving
principle and cause.
In beautiful things
he saw Beauty itself,
and through his vestiges imprinted on creation
he followed his Beloved everywhere,
making from all things a ladder
by which he could climb up
and embrace him who is utterly desirable.
With a feeling of unprecedented devotion
he savored
in each and every creature—
as in so many rivulets—
that Goodness
which is their fountain-source.
And he perceived a heavenly harmony
in the consonance
of powers and activities
God has given them,
and like the prophet David
sweetly exhorted them to praise the Lord.

Jesus Christ crucified always rested like a bundle of myrrh in the bosom of Francis's soul, and he longed to be totally transformed into him by the fire of ecstatic love. As a sign of his special devotion to him, Francis spent the time from the feast of the Epiphany through forty successive days—that period when Christ was hidden in the desert—secluded in a lonely place, shut up in a cell, with as little food and drink as possible, fasting, praying and praising God without interruption. He was drawn to Christ with such fervent love, and the Beloved returned such intimate love to him that God's servant always seemed to feel the presence of his Savior before his eyes, as he once intimately revealed to his companions. His very marrow burned with love for the sacrament of the Lord's Body, and he was overcome by wonder at such loving condescension and such condescending love. He received Holy Communion often and so devoutly that he made others devout also, for at the sweet taste of the spotless Lamb he was often rapt in ecstasy as if drunk in the Spirit.

He embraced the mother of the Lord Jesus with an indescribable love because she had made the Lord of Majesty our brother and because through her we have obtained mercy. After Christ he put all his trust in her and made her his advocate and that of his friars. In her honor he used to fast with great devotion from the feast of the Apostles Peter and Paul to the feast of the Assumption. He was joined in a bond of inseparable love to the angels who burn with a marvelous fire to be rapt out of themselves into God and to inflame the souls of the elect. Out of devotion to the angels he used to spend the forty days after the Assumption of the glorious Virgin in fasting and continual prayer. Because of the ardent zeal he had for the salvation of all, he was devoted with a special love to blessed Michael the Archangel in view of his ministry of presenting souls to God.

In remembering all the saints who are like fiery stones, he burned with a divine fire and embraced with great devotion all the apostles, especially Peter and Paul, because of the ardent love they had toward Christ. Out of reverence and love for them he dedicated to the Lord a special fast of forty days.

> The poor man of Christ
> had only two mites,
> namely his body and his soul,
> which he could give away in generous charity.
> But out of love of Christ
> he offered them so continuously
> that he seemed to be constantly immolating
> his body
> through the rigor of fasting
> and his spirit
> through the ardor of his desire,
> sacrificing a holocaust in the outer courtyard
> and burning incense
> in the interior of the temple.

The ecstatic devotion of his charity so bore him aloft into the divine that his loving kindness was enlarged and extended to all who shared with him in nature and grace. Since his heartfelt devotedness had made him a brother to all other creatures, it is no wonder that the charity of Christ made him more than a brother to those who are stamped with the image of their Creator and redeemed with the blood of their Maker. He would not consider himself a friend of Christ unless he cared for the souls whom Christ redeemed. He used to say that nothing should be preferred to the salvation of souls, offering as the supreme proof of this the fact that it was for souls that the only-begotten Son of God deigned to hang on the cross. This is the reason for his struggles in prayer, his untiring preaching tours and his lack of measure in giving example.

Therefore when he was reproached for his excessive severity toward himself, he would reply that he was given as an example for others. For although his innocent flesh, which always of its own accord subjected itself to the spirit, had no need for any penitential scourging, he nevertheless inflicted punishment and burdens on it as an example, keeping to the hard paths for the sake of others. For he used to say: "'If I speak with the tongues of men and angels, but have not charity' (1 Cor. 13:1–3) and do not show examples of virtue to my neighbors, it is little use to them and nothing to myself."

> In the fervent fire
> of his charity
> he strove to emulate
> the glorious triumph of the holy martyrs
> in whom
> the flame of love could not be extinguished
> nor courage be weakened.
> Set on fire, therefore,
> by that perfect charity which drives out fear,
> he longed to offer to the Lord
> his own life as a living sacrifice
> in the flames of martyrdom

so that he might repay Christ,
who died for us,
and inspire others to divine love.

In the sixth year of his conversion, burning with a desire of martyrdom, he decided to cross the sea to the regions of Syria in order to preach penance and the Christian faith to the Saracens and other infidels. When he had boarded a ship to go there, he was driven by contrary winds to land in the region of Dalmatia. He spent some time there and could not find a ship that would cross the sea at that time. Feeling that he had been cheated of his desire, he begged some sailors who were going to Ancona to take him with them for the love of God. When they obstinately refused because he could not pay his expenses, the man of God, trusting completely in the Lord's goodness, stowed away on the boat with his companion. A certain man came on board, sent by God for his poor man, as it is believed, who brought with him the necessary provisions. He called one of the crew who feared God and told him: "Keep all these things faithfully for the poor friars who are hiding on board and give them to them in a friendly fashion when they need them." And it so happened that, when the crew could not land anywhere for a number of days because of the force of the winds, they ate all their provisions and all that was left over was the alms supernaturally given to the poor Francis. Although this was only a very small amount, by God's power it was multiplied so much that while they were delayed at sea for many days by the continuing storm, it fully provided for their needs all the way to Ancona. Therefore when the sailors saw that they had escaped many threats of death, as men who had experienced the horrible dangers of the sea and had seen the wonderful works of the Lord in the deep, they thanked Almighty God, who always shows himself wonderful and lovable in his friends and servants.

When he left the coast, he began to walk over the land and to sow in it the seed of salvation, reaping a fruitful harvest. But the fruit of martyrdom had so attracted his heart that he desired a precious death for the sake of Christ more intensely than all the merits from the virtues. So he took the road to Morocco in order to preach the Gospel of Christ to the Miramamolin and his people, hoping to attain in this way the palm of martyrdom he so strongly desired. He was carried along with such a great desire that although he was physically weak, he used to run ahead of his companion on the trip in his haste to achieve his purpose, flying along, as if drunk in spirit. But when he had gone as far as Spain, by God's design, which had more important things in store for him, he was overtaken by a serious illness which hindered him from achieving what he desired. Realizing, then, that his physical life was still necessary for the children he had begotten, the man of God, although he considered death as gain for himself, returned to feed the sheep entrusted to his care.

The ardor of his charity urged his spirit on toward martyrdom, and he tried to set out to the infidels yet a third time, hoping to shed his blood for the spread of the faith in the Trinity. In the thirteenth year of his conversion, he traveled to the regions of

Syria, constantly exposing himself to many dangers in order to reach the presence of the Soldan of Babylon. For at that time there was a fierce war between the Christians and the Saracens, with their camps situated in close quarters opposite each other in the field so that there was no way of passing from one to the other without danger of death. A cruel edict had been issued by the Soldan that whoever would bring back the head of a Christian would receive as a reward a gold piece. But Francis, the intrepid knight of Christ, hoping to be able to achieve his purpose, decided to make the journey, not terrified by the fear of death, but rather drawn by desire for it. After praying, strengthened by the Lord, he confidently chanted the verse of the Prophet: "Even if I should walk in the midst of the shadow of death, I shall not fear evil because you are with me" (Ps. 23:4).

He took with him as his companion a friar named Illuminato, a virtuous and enlightened man. When he had begun his journey, he came upon two lambs. Overjoyed to see them, the holy man said to his companion: "Trust in the Lord, brother, for the Gospel text is being fulfilled in us: 'Behold, I am sending you forth like sheep in the midst of wolves'" (Matt. 10:16). When they proceeded farther, the Saracen sentries fell upon them like wolves swiftly overtaking sheep, savagely seized the servants of God and cruelly and contemptuously dragged them away, insulting them, beating them and putting them in chains. Finally, after they had been maltreated in many ways and were exhausted, by divine providence they were led to the Soldan, just as the man of God wished. When that ruler inquired by whom, why and how they had been sent and how they got there, Francis, Christ's servant, answered with an intrepid heart that he had been sent not by man but by the Most High God in order to point out to him and his people the way of salvation and to announce the Gospel of truth. He preached to the Soldan the Triune God and the one Savior of all, Jesus Christ, with such constancy of mind, such courage of soul and such fervor of spirit that the words of the Gospel were clearly and truly fulfilled in him: "I will give you utterance and wisdom which all your adversaries will not be able to resist or answer back" (Luke 21:15).

When the Soldan saw this admirable fervor of spirit and courage in the man of God, he willingly listened to him and earnestly invited him to stay longer with him. Inspired from heaven, Christ's servant said: "If you wish to be converted to Christ along with your people, I will most gladly stay with you for love of him. But if you hesitate to abandon the law of Mahomet for the faith of Christ, then command that an enormous fire be lit and I will walk into the fire along with your priests so that you will recognize which faith deserves to be held as the holier and more certain." The Soldan answered him: "I do not believe that any of my priests would be willing to expose himself to the fire to defend his faith or to undergo any kind of torment." For he had seen immediately one of his priests, a man full of authority and years, slipping away from his view when he heard Francis's words. The saint said to the Soldan: "If you wish to promise that if I come out of the fire unharmed, you and your people will come over to the worship of Christ, then I will enter the fire alone. And if I shall be burned, you must attribute it to my sins. But if God's power protects me, you will acknowledge 'Christ the power and wisdom of God' (1 Cor. 1:24) as 'true God' (John 17:3) and the 'Savior' (John 4:42) of all." The Soldan replied that he did not dare to accept this choice because he feared a revolt among his people. Nevertheless he offered Francis many valuable gifts, which the man of God, greedy not for worldly possessions but for the salvation of souls, spurned as if they were dirt. Seeing that the holy man so completely despised worldly possessions, the Soldan was filled with admiration and developed an even greater respect for him. Although he refused, or perhaps did not dare, to come over to the Christian faith, he nevertheless devoutly asked Christ's servant to accept the gifts and give them to the Christian poor or to churches for the Soldan's salvation. But Francis would in no way accept them because he was accustomed to flee from the burden of money and he did not see that true piety had taken root in the Soldan's soul.

When he saw that he was making no progress in converting these people and that he could not achieve his purpose, namely martyrdom, he went back to the lands of the faithful, as he was advised by a divine revelation.

> Thus by the kindness of God
> and the merits of the virtue of the holy man,
> it came about
> mercifully and remarkably
> that the friend of Christ

sought with all his strength
to die for him
and yet could not achieve it.
Thus he was not deprived
of the merit of his desired martyrdom
and was spared
to be honored in the future
with a unique privilege.
Thus it came about
that the divine fire
burned still more perfectly in his heart
so that later it steamed forth clearly
in his flesh.
O truly blessed man,
whose flesh,
although not cut down by a tyrant's steel,
was yet not deprived
of bearing a likeness of the Lamb that was slain!
O, truly and fully blessed man, I say,
whose life
"the persecutor's sword did not take away,
and who yet did not lose the palm of
    martyrdom"!

Chapter 10

On His Zeal for Prayer and the Power of His Prayer

Realizing that while he was in the body
he was exiled from the Lord,
since he was made totally insensible
to earthly desires
through his love of Christ,
the servant of Christ Francis
strove to keep his spirit
in the presence of God,
by praying without ceasing
so that he might not be without the comfort
of his Beloved.
Prayer was a delight
to this contemplative
who had already become
a fellow citizen of the angels
and who, making the rounds of the heavenly
    mansions,
sought with burning desire
that Beloved
from whom he was separated
only by the wall of the flesh.
Prayer was a support
to this worker;

for in everything which he did,
distrusting his own effort
and trusting in God's loving concern,
he cast his care completely upon the Lord
in urgent prayers to him.
He used to state firmly
that the grace of prayer
was to be desired above all else
by a religious man,
believing that without it no one could prosper
   in God's service.
He used whatever means he could
to arouse his friars
to be zealous in prayer.
For whether walking or sitting,
inside or outside,
working or resting,
he was so intent on prayer
that he seemed to have dedicated to it
not only his heart and body
but also all his effort and time.

He was accustomed not to pass over negligently any visitation of the Spirit. When it was granted, he followed it, and as long as the Lord allowed, he enjoyed the sweetness offered him. When he was on a journey and felt the breathing of the divine Spirit, letting his companions go on ahead, he would stand still and render this new inspiration fruitful, not receiving the grace in vain. Many times he was lifted up in ecstatic contemplation so that, rapt out of himself and experiencing what is beyond human understanding, he was unaware of what went on about him. Once when he was traveling through Borgo San Sepolcro, a heavily populated town, and was riding on an ass because of physical weakness, crowds rushed to meet him out of devotion. He was pulled and held back by them, pushed and touched all over; yet he seemed insensible to it all and noticed nothing at all of what was going on around him, as if he were a lifeless corpse. Long after he had passed the town and left the crowds, he came to a house of lepers; and that contemplator of heavenly things, as if returning from far away, solicitously inquired when they would be approaching Borgo San Sepolcro. His mind was so fixed on heavenly splendors that he was not aware of the varieties of place, time and people that he passed. That this happened to him often was confirmed by the repeated experience of his companions.

He had learned in prayer that the presence of the Holy Spirit for which he longed was granted more intimately to those who invoke him, the more the Holy Spirit found them withdrawn from the noise of worldly affairs. Therefore seeking out lonely places, he used to go to deserted areas and abandoned churches to pray at night. There he often endured horrible struggles with devils who fought with him physically, trying to distract him from his commitment to prayer. But armed with heavenly weapons, the more vehemently he was attacked by the enemy, the more courageous he became in practicing virtue and the more fervent in prayer, saying confidently to Christ: "Under the shadow of your wings, protect me from the face of the wicked who have attacked me" (Ps. 17:8-9). To the devils he said: "Do whatever you want to me, you malicious and deceitful spirits! For you cannot do anything except insofar as God relaxes his hold on you. And I am ready and happy to endure everything that his hand should decide to let loose on me." Such firmness of mind the devils could not bear, and they retreated in confusion.

When the man of God was left alone and at peace, he would fill the groves with sighs, sprinkle the ground with tears, strike his breast with his fist and, having found there a kind of secret hiding place, converse with his Lord. There he would answer his Judge, there he would entreat his Father, there he would entertain his Friend; and there also on several occasions the friars who were devoutly observing him heard him groan aloud, imploring the divine mercy for sinners and weeping for the Lord's passion as if it were there before his eyes. There he was seen praying at night, with his hands outstretched in the form of a cross, his whole body lifted up from the ground and surrounded by a sort of shining cloud. The extraordinary illumination around his body was a witness to the wonderful light that shone within his soul. There also, as is proven by certain evidence, the unknown and hidden secrets of divine wisdom were opened up to him, although he never spoke of them outside except when the love of Christ urged him and the good of his neighbor demanded. For he used to say: "It happens that if a person loses some priceless thing for the sake of a small gain, he easily provokes the one who gave it not to give again."

When he returned from his private prayers, by which he was changed almost into another man, he used to expend the greatest effort to be like the others so that what he might show outwardly would not deprive him of his inner reward because of the glow of human attention. When he was suddenly moved in public by a visitation from the Lord, he would always put something between himself and the bystanders, lest he make common the sight of the Bridegroom's intimate embraces. When he prayed with the friars, he completely avoided all spluttering, groaning, deep sighs or external movements, either because he loved to keep secrecy or because he had withdrawn into his interior and was totally carried into God. He often told his companions: "When a servant of God receives a divine visitation in prayer, he should say: 'Lord, you have sent this consolation from heaven to me an unworthy sinner, and I entrust it to your keeping because I feel that I am a robber of your treasure.' When he returns from his prayer, he should show himself as a poor man and a sinner, as if he had obtained no new grace."

Once when the man of God was praying at the Portiuncula, it happened that the bishop of Assisi came to visit him as he often did. As soon as he entered the friars' place, he went more abruptly than he should to the cell where Christ's servant was praying, and after knocking at the door, was about to enter when he put his head in and saw the saint praying. Suddenly the bishop began to tremble, his limbs stiffened, he lost his voice, and all at once by the will of God he was cast outside with force and driven some distance backward. Shaken, the bishop hurried to the friars, and when God had restored his speech, with his first words and as best he could he confessed his fault.

Another time it happened that the abbot of the monastery of St.

Justin in the diocese of Perugia met Christ's servant on the road. When he saw him, the devout abbot quickly got down from his horse to show reverence to the man of God and to confer with him a bit on the welfare of his soul. Finally, after a pleasant conversation, the abbot, as he was leaving, humbly asked Francis to pray for him. The beloved man of God replied: "I will be happy to pray for you." When the abbot had gone a little way, the faithful Francis said to his companion: "Wait a little, brother, because I wish to pay the debt as I promised." As Francis prayed, suddenly the abbot felt in his spirit an unusual warmth and sweetness such as he had never before experienced, so much so that he was rapt in ecstasy and totally lost himself in God. He remained so for a short while, and when he came back to himself, recognized the power of St. Francis in prayer. After that he always burned with a greater love for the Order and related the event to many as a miracle.

The holy man was accustomed to recite the canonical hours with no less reverence than devotion. For although he suffered from an illness of the eyes, stomach, spleen and liver, nevertheless he did not want to lean against a wall while he chanted the psalms; but he said the complete hours standing erect and with head uncovered, not letting his eyes wander around and not clipping the syllables short. If he were on a journey, he would stop at the right time and never omitted this reverent and holy practice because of rain. For he used to say: "If the body requires quiet to eat its food, which along with itself will become the food of worms, with what peace and tranquillity should not the soul receive the food of life?"

He thought that he had seriously offended if, when he was at prayer, his mind wandered over vain imaginations. When something like this happened, he did not wait to confess it so that he could atone for it immediately. He so put his zeal into practice that he rarely was bothered by "flies" of this kind.

One Lent he was whittling a little cup to occupy his spare moments and to prevent them from being wasted. When he was reciting Terce, it came to his mind and distracted him a little. Moved by fervor of spirit, he burned the cup in the fire, saying: "I will sacrifice this to the Lord, whose sacrifice it has impeded."

He used to say the psalms with such attention of mind and spirit, as if he had God present. When the Lord's name occurred in the psalms, he seemed to lick his lips because of its sweetness. He wanted to honor with special reverence the Lord's name not only when thought but also when spoken and written. He once persuaded the friars to gather all pieces of paper wherever found and to place them in a clean place so that if that sacred name happened to be written there, it would not be trodden underfoot. When he pronounced or heard the name "Jesus," he was filled with joy interiorly and seemed to be altered exteriorly as if some honey-sweet flavor had transformed his taste or some harmonious sound had transformed his hearing.

It happened in the third year before his death that he decided, in order to arouse devotion, to celebrate at Greccio with the greatest possible solemnity the memory of the birth of the Child Jesus. So that this would not be considered a type of novelty, he petitioned for and obtained permission from the Supreme Pontiff. He had a crib prepared, hay carried in and an ox and an ass led to the place. The friars were summoned, the people came, the forest resounded with their voices and that venerable night was rendered brilliant and solemn by a multitude of bright lights and by resonant and harmonious hymns of praise. The man of God stood before the crib, filled with affection, bathed in tears and overflowing with joy. A solemn Mass was celebrated over the crib, with Francis as deacon chanting the holy Gospel. Then he preached to the people standing about concerning the birth of the poor King, whom, when he wished to name him, he called in his tender love, the Child of Bethlehem.

A certain virtuous and truthful knight, Sir John of Greccio, who had abandoned worldly military activity out of love of Christ and had become an intimate friend of the man of God, claimed that he saw a beautiful little boy asleep in the crib and that the blessed father Francis embraced it in both of his arms and seemed to wake it from sleep.

> Not only does the holiness of the witness
> make credible
> this vision of the devout knight,
> but also the truth it expresses
> proves its validity
> and the subsequent miracles confirm it.
> For Francis's example
> when considered by the world
> is capable of arousing
> the hearts of those who are sluggish
> in the faith of Christ.

The hay from the crib
was kept by the people
and miraculously cured sick animals
and drove away different kinds of pestilence.
Thus God glorified his servant in every way
and demonstrated the efficacy
of his holy prayer
by the evident signs
of wonderful miracles.

Chapter 11

On His Understanding of Scripture and His Spirit of Prophecy

His unwearied application to prayer
along with his continual exercise of virtue
had led the man of God
to such serenity of mind
that although he had no skill in Sacred Scripture
acquired through study,
his intellect,
illumined by the brilliance of eternal light,
probed the depths of Scripture
with remarkable acumen.
Free from all stain,
his genius penetrated the hidden depths of the
    mysteries,
and where the scholarship of the teacher
stands outside,
the affection of the lover
entered within.

At times he would read the sacred books, and what he had once put in his mind he imprinted firmly on his memory. It was not in vain that this attentive mind grasped something he heard, for he would meditate on it with love and continued devotion. Once the friars asked him whether he was pleased that the learned men who had by that time been received into the Order should devote themselves to the study of Sacred Scripture. He replied: "I am indeed pleased, as long as they do not neglect application to prayer, after the example of Christ, of whom we read that he prayed more than he read, and as long as they study not only in order to know what they should say but in order to practice what they have heard and when they have put it into practice them- selves to propose it to others likewise. I want my friars," he said, "to be disciples of the Gospel and to progress in knowledge of the truth in such a way as to increase in pure simplicity without separating the simplicity of the dove from the wisdom of the ser- pent which our eminent Teacher joined together in a statement from his own blessed lips."

Francis was once consulted at Siena by a religious who was a doctor of theology about certain questions that were difficult to understand. He brought to light the secrets of divine wisdom with such clarity in teaching that the learned man was absolutely dumbfounded and responded with admiration: "Truly the theol- ogy of this holy father, borne aloft, as it were, on the wings of purity and contemplation, is a soaring eagle; but our learning crawls on its belly on the ground." Although he was unskilled in speaking, he was filled with knowledge and explained doubtful questions and brought hidden things to light. Nor should it sound odd that the holy man should have received from God an understanding of the Scriptures, since through his perfect imita- tion of Christ he carried into practice the truth described in them and, through the abundant anointing of the Holy Spirit, had their Teacher within himself in his heart.

The spirit of prophecy, too, so shone forth in him that he foresaw the future and had knowledge of the secrets of the heart. He was aware of things absent as if they were present, and he miraculously appeared present to those who were absent. At the time when the Christian army was besieging Damietta, the man of God was there, armed with faith and not weapons. When on the day of the battle he heard that the Christians were preparing to fight, Christ's servant sighed heavily and said to his companion: "The Lord has shown me that if the battle takes place, it will not go well for the Christians. But if I tell them this, I will be considered a fool. If I remain silent, I will not escape my conscience. What therefore seems best to you?" His companion replied: "Brother, consider it unimportant to be judged by men, for this won't be the first time you pass for a fool. Unburden your conscience, and fear God rather than men." When he heard this, the herald of Christ jumped to his feet and went to the Christians with his salutary warnings, forbidding the battle and announcing their defeat. They took his truth for a fairy tale, hardened their hearts and refused to turn back. They advanced and engaged the enemy in battle, with the result that the whole Christian army was turned to flight, bearing away disgrace rather than triumph. The Christian forces suffered such heavy losses that there were about six thousand dead or captured. From this it was abundantly clear that the wisdom of this poor man was not to be scorned, since sometimes the soul of a just man will declare truths more clearly than seven sentinels searching the horizon from a height (Eccl. 37:14).

Another time, after his return from overseas, he went to Celano to preach; and a certain knight invited him to dinner with humble devotion and with great insistence. So he came to the knight's home, and the whole family rejoiced at the coming of the poor guests. Before they took any food, the saint offered prayers and praise to God as was his custom, standing with his eyes raised to heaven. When he finished his prayer, he called his kind host aside and confidentially told him: "Look, brother host, conquered by your prayers, I have entered your house to eat. Now heed my warnings quickly because you will not dine here but elsewhere. Confess your sins right now, contrite with the sorrow of true repentance; and let nothing remain in you that you do not reveal in a true confession. The Lord will reward you today because you have received his poor with such devotion." The man heeded the saint's words at once; and laying bare all of his sins in confession to Francis's companion, he put his house in order and did everything in his power to prepare for death. At length they went to the table; and while the others began to eat, suddenly their host breathed forth his spirit, carried away by sudden death as the man of God had foretold. So it happened that in recompense for the kindness of his hospitality "he received a prophet's reward because he had received a prophet," according to the word of Truth (Matt. 10:41). Through the holy man's prophecy, that devout knight prepared himself for a sudden death so that, protected by the armor of repentance, he escaped perpetual damnation and entered into the eternal dwellings.

At the time when the holy man was lying ill at Rieti, a canon by the name of Gedeon, a dissolute and worldly man, became seriously ill and took to his bed. He had himself carried to Francis, and together with those present, he tearfully begged to be blessed with the sign of the cross. Francis answered: "Since you lived in the past according to the desires of the flesh, not fearing God's judgments, how will I make the sign of the cross over you? However, because of the devout requests of those pleading for you, I will make the sign of the cross over you in the name of the Lord. Nevertheless, realize that you will suffer more seriously if, after being delivered, you return to your vomit. Because of the sin of ingratitude worse things than before are inflicted." The moment he made the sign of the cross over him, the man who had lain there crippled arose healthy and broke out in praise of God, saying: "I am freed." But the bones of his loins made a noise which many heard as if dry sticks were being broken with the hand. After a short time had elapsed, forgetful of God, he gave his body again to impurity. One evening when he had dined at the home of another canon and was sleeping there that night, suddenly the roof of the house fell down on them all. The others escaped death and only that wretched man was trapped and killed. Therefore by the just judgment of God, "the last state of that man became worse than the first" (Matt. 12:45) on account of his vice of ingratitude and his contempt for God, when he should have been grateful for the forgiveness he had received. A crime that is repeated is doubly offensive.

Another time, a noble woman, devoted to God, came to the saint to explain her trouble to him and ask for help. She had a very cruel husband who opposed her serving Christ. So she begged the saint to pray for him so that God in his goodness would soften his

heart. When he heard this, he said to her: "Go in peace, and without any doubt be assured that your husband will soon be a comfort to you." And he added: "Tell him on God's part and my own,
that now is the time of mercy, and afterwards of justice." After
receiving a blessing, the woman went home, found her husband
and delivered the message. The Holy Spirit came upon him, making him a new man and inducing him to answer with gentleness:
"My lady, let us serve the Lord and save our souls." At the suggestion of his holy wife, they lived a celibate life for many years, and
both passed away to the Lord on the same day.

> The power of the prophetic spirit
> in the man of God
> was certainly extraordinary,
> which restored vigor to dried-up limbs
> and impressed piety on hardened hearts.
> The lucidity of his spirit
> was no less an object of wonder;
> for he could foresee future events
> and even probe the secrets of conscience,
> as if he were another Elisha,
> who had acquired the twofold spirit of Elijah.

On one occasion he told a friend at Siena what would happen to
him at the end of his life. Now when the learned man mentioned
above, who consulted him at one time about the Scriptures, heard
of this, he asked the holy father in doubt whether he had really
said what the man had claimed. Francis not only confirmed that
he had said this but besides foretold to this learned man who was

so eager to know another's future the circumstances of his own end. To impress this with greater certainty on his heart, Francis miraculously revealed to him a certain secret scruple of conscience which the man had and which he had never disclosed to any living person; and he relieved him of it by his sound advice. The truth of all this was confirmed by the fact that this religious eventually died just as Christ's servant had foretold.

When he was returning from overseas with Brother Leonard of Assisi as his companion, it happened that he was riding for a while on a donkey because he was fatigued and weary. But his companion, following along behind, was not a little weary himself and giving in to human weakness began to say within himself: "His parents and mine never played together as equals. And look—he is riding and I am on foot leading his donkey." While he was thinking this, the holy man all at once got down from the donkey and said: "Brother, it is not right that I should ride and you should go on foot, for in the world you were more noble and more powerful than I." The friar was dumbfounded at this and blushed, realizing he had been caught. He fell at Francis's feet and, bathed in tears, exposed his thought naked to the saint and begged his forgiveness.

A certain friar, devoted to God and to Christ's servant, frequently turned over in his heart the idea that whoever was held in the holy man's intimate affection would be worthy of God's grace and whomever he excluded from his intimacy would not be regarded among the elect by God. He was obsessed by the repeated pressure of this thought and intensely longed for the intimate friendship of the man of God, but never revealed the secret of his heart to anyone. The devoted father called him and spoke sweetly to him as follows: "Let no thought trouble you, my son, because among those who are especially dear to me I hold you most dear, and I gladly lavish upon you my friendship and love." The friar was amazed at this and became even more devoted to Francis. He not only grew in his love for the holy man, but also through the grace of the Holy Spirit he was filled with still greater gifts.

While Francis was staying on Mount La Verna, secluded in his cell, one of his companions greatly desired to have some of the Lord's words briefly noted down and written in the saint's own hand. By this means he believed he would escape from a serious temptation that was vexing him, not of the flesh but of the spirit, or at very least that he would bear it more easily. Languishing with this desire, he was in a state of internal anxiety because, overcome with embarrassment, he did not dare to disclose the matter to the venerable father. But what man did not tell Francis the Holy Spirit revealed to him. He ordered this previously mentioned friar to bring him some ink and paper; and he wrote down the Praises of the Lord in his own hand as the friar desired and, finally, a blessing for him, saying: "Take this slip of paper and guard it carefully until the day of your death." The friar took the gift he so much desired and immediately his temptation was put to flight. The writing was preserved, and since it later worked miracles, it became a witness to the power of Francis.

There was a certain friar, eminent in holiness and outstanding in his manner of life, as far as it seemed outwardly, but who did everything very much in his own way. He spent all his time in prayer and observed silence with such strictness that he used to confess not with words but with signs. It happened that the holy father came to that place, saw the friar and spoke to the other friars about him. When they all commended and praised him highly, the man of God replied: "Brothers, let him alone and do not praise to me what the devil has wrought in him. Know in truth that it is a temptation of the devil and a fraudulent deception." The friars took this harshly, judging that it was impossible that contrivances of fraud could paint themselves over with so many signs of perfection. But not many days later this friar left the Order, and the brilliance of the interior insight with which the man of God perceived the secrets of his heart became abundantly clear.

> In this way
> Francis foretold with unchanging truth
> the fall
> of many who seemed to stand firm
> and the conversion to Christ
> of many who were perverse.
> He seemed to have approached
> in contemplation
> the mirror of the eternal light,
> in whose marvelous splendor
> the gaze of his mind saw
> things that happened at a physical distance
> as if they were present.

Once while his vicar was holding a chapter, Francis was praying in his cell, as the go-between and mediator between the friars and God. One of them, hiding behind the mantle of some excuse, would not submit himself to the discipline of obedience. Seeing this in spirit, the holy man called one of the friars and said to him: "Brother, I saw the devil on the back of that disobedient friar, holding him tightly by the neck. Driven by such a rider, he had spurned the bridle of obedience and was giving rein to his own inclination. But when I prayed to God for the friar, the devil suddenly went away in confusion. Go and tell the friar to submit his neck to the yoke of holy obedience without delay!" Admonished by this intermediary, the friar immediately was converted to God and cast himself humbly at the feet of the vicar.

Another time it happened that two friars came from a distance to the hermitage of Greccio to see the man of God and to receive his blessing, which they had desired for a long time. When they came and did not find him, because he had already withdrawn and gone to his cell, they went away quite desolate. And behold, as they were leaving, although he could not have known anything of their arrival or departure through any human perception, he came out of his cell contrary to his custom, shouted after them and blessed them in Christ's name with the sign of the cross, just as they had desired.

Two friars once came from the Terra di Lavoro, the elder of whom had given much scandal to the younger. When they reached the father, he asked the younger friar how his companion had behaved toward him on the way. The friar replied: "Quite well"; but Francis said: "Be careful, brother, not to tell a lie under the pretext of humility. For I know, I know; but wait a little and

you will see." The friar was amazed at how he could have known
in spirit what had happened at a distance. Now not many days
after, the one who had given scandal to his brother left the Order
in contempt and went out into the world. He did not ask the
father's forgiveness nor accept the discipline of correction as he
should. In that single fall, two things shone forth clearly: the
equity of the divine judgment and the penetrating power of the
spirit of prophecy.

> How he appeared as present
> to those who were absent,
> through God's power,
> becomes evidently clear
> from what was said above,
> if we recall to mind
> how he appeared to the friars,
> although absent,
> transfigured in a fiery chariot,
> and how he presented himself
> at the Chapter of Arles
> in the image of a cross.
> We ought to believe
> that this was done by divine providence
> so that from his miraculous appearance in
>   bodily presence
> it might clearly shine forth
> how present and open his spirit was
> to the light of eternal wisdom,
> which is mobile beyond all motion,
> reaching everywhere because of its purity.

And spreading through the nations
into holy souls
it makes them prophets and friends of God.
The exalted Teacher
is accustomed to open his mysteries
to the simple and the little ones
as was first seen
in the case of David, the most distinguished of
    the prophets,
and afterwards in Peter, the prince of the
    apostles,
and finally in Francis, the little poor man of
    Christ.
Although these were simple men
unskilled in learning,
they were made illustrious
by the teaching of the Holy Spirit.
One was a shepherd
who pastured the Synagogue,
the flock God had led out of Egypt;
the other was a fisherman
who filled the net of the Church
with many kinds of believers.
The last was a merchant
who bought the pearl of the Gospel life,
selling and giving away all he had
for the sake of Christ.

Chapter 12

On the Efficacy of His Preaching and His Grace of Healing

Francis,
the truly faithful servant and minister of Christ,
in order to do everything
faithfully and perfectly,
used to direct his efforts chiefly
to the exercise of those virtues
which by the inspiration of the Holy Spirit
he knew pleased God more.
In this matter it happened
that he fell into a great struggle
over a doubt which,
after many days of prayer,
he proposed for resolution
to the friars who were close to him.
"What do you think, brothers,
what do you judge better?
That I should spend my time in prayer
or that I should go about preaching?
I am a poor little man,
simple and unskilled in speech;
I have received a greater grace of prayer than of
    speaking.
Also in prayer there seems to be a profit

and the accumulation of graces,
but in preaching
the distribution of gifts already received from
    heaven.
In prayer
our interior affections are purified
and we are united
with the one true and highest good
as well as strengthened in virtue;
in preaching,
we get dust on our spiritual feet,
distraction over many things and relaxation of
    discipline.
Finally, in prayer
we address God,
listen to him
and dwell among the angels
as if we were living an angelic life;
in preaching
we must think, see, say and hear
human things,
adapting ourselves to them
as if we were living on a human level,
for men and among men.
But there is one thing to the contrary,
that seems to outweigh all these considerations
before God,
namely that the only begotten Son of God,
who is the highest wisdom,
came down from the bosom of the Father
for the sake of souls

in order to instruct the world with his example
and to speak the word of salvation to men,
whom he would redeem
with the price of his sacred blood,
cleanse with its washing
and nourish with its draft,
holding back for himself absolutely nothing
that he could freely give for our salvation.
And because we should do everything
according to the pattern shown to us in him
as on the heights of the mountain,
it seems more pleasing to God
that I interrupt my quiet
and go out to labor."
When he had mulled over these words
for many days with his friars,
he could not perceive with certainty
which of these he should choose
as more acceptable to Christ.
Although he understood extraordinary things
through the spirit of prophecy,
this question he could not resolve with
    certainty
on his own.
But God's providence had a better plan,
that the merit of preaching would be shown
by a revelation from heaven,
thus preserving the humility of Christ's servant.
He was not ashamed
to ask advice in small matters
from those under him,

true Friar Minor that he was,
though he had learned great things
from the supreme Teacher.
He was accustomed
to search out with special eagerness
how and in what way
he could serve God more perfectly
according to God's good pleasure.
As long as he lived
this was his supreme philosophy,
this his supreme desire,
to inquire from the wise and the simple,
the perfect and the imperfect,
the young and the old,
how he could more effectively reach
the summit of perfection.

Choosing, therefore, two of the friars, he sent them to Brother Silvester—who had seen the cross coming out from his mouth and in those days spent his time in continuous prayer on the mountain above Assisi—that Silvester might ask God to resolve his doubt over this matter and send him the answer in God's name. He also asked the holy virgin Clare to consult with the purest and simplest of the virgins living under her rule and to pray herself with the other sisters in order to seek the Lord's will in this matter. Through the miraculous revelation of the Holy Spirit, the venerable priest and the virgin dedicated to God came to the same conclusion: that it was God's good pleasure that Francis should preach as the herald of Christ. When the two fri-

ars returned and told him God's will as they had received it, he at
once rose, girded himself and without the slightest delay took to
the roads. He went with such fervor to carry out the divine command and he ran along so swiftly that the hand of God seemed
to be upon him, giving him new strength from heaven.

When he was approaching Bevagna, he came to a spot where a
large flock of birds of various kinds had come together. When
God's saint saw them, he quickly ran to the spot and greeted
them as if they were endowed with reason. They all became alert
and turned toward him, and those perched in the trees bent their
heads as he approached them and in an uncommon way directed
their attention to him. He went right up to them and solicitously
urged them to listen to the word of God, saying: "Oh birds, my
brothers, you have a great obligation to praise your Creator, who
clothed you in feathers and gave you wings to fly with, provided
you with the pure air and cares for you without any worry on
your part." While he was saying this and similar things to them,
the birds showed their joy in a remarkable fashion: they began to
stretch their necks, extend their wings, open their beaks and gaze
at him attentively. He went through their midst with amazing fervor of spirit, brushing against them with his tunic. Yet none of
them moved from the spot until the man of God made the sign of
the cross and gave them his blessing and permission to leave;
then they all flew away together. His companions waiting on the
road saw all these things. When he returned to them, that pure
and simple man began to accuse himself of negligence because
he had not preached to the birds before.

From there he went preaching through the neighboring districts and came to a village by the name of Alviano. When the people were gathered, he called for silence, but could scarcely be heard above the racket made by some swallows that were building nests there. In the hearing of all the people, the man of God addressed them and said: "My sister swallows, it is time now for me to speak because you have said enough already. Listen to the word of God and keep silence until his message is finished." As if they had been able to understand him, they suddenly became silent and did not move from that place until the whole sermon was finished. All who saw this were filled with amazement and glorified God. News of this miracle spread around everywhere, enkindling reverence for the saint and devotion for the faith.

In the city of Parma, a certain student, an excellent young man, was diligently studying with his companions when he was distracted by the troublesome chattering of a swallow. He began to say to his companions: "This must be one of those swallows that kept bothering the man of God Francis when he was once preaching, until he had to shut them up." He turned to the swallow and said confidently: "In the name of God's servant Francis, I command you to come to me and to be silent at once." When it heard the name of Francis, it immediately became silent, as if it really had been trained by the teaching of the man of God, and entrusted itself to the student's hands as if to a safe refuge. The amazed student immediately set it free and never heard its chattering again.

Another time, when God's servant was preaching on the

seashore at Gaeta, out of devotion crowds rushed upon him in order to touch him. Horrified at such popularity, he jumped all alone into a small boat that was drawn up on the shore. The boat began to move as if it had both intellect and motion of itself and, without the help of any oars, glided away from the shore, to the wonderment of all who witnessed it. When it had gone out some distance into the deep water, it stood motionless on the waves, as long as the holy man preached to the attentive crowd on the shore. When, after hearing the sermon, seeing the miracle and receiving his blessing, the crowd went away and would no longer trouble him, the boat returned to land on its own power.

> Who, then, would be
> so obstinate and lacking in piety
> as to look down upon the preaching of Francis?
> By his remarkable power,
> not only creatures lacking reason learned
> > obedience
> but even inanimate objects served him
> when he preached,
> as if they had life.
> The Spirit of the Lord
> who had anointed and sent him
> and also Christ,
> the power and the wisdom of God,
> were with their servant Francis
> wherever he went
> so that he might abound
> with words of sound teaching
> and shine

with miracles of great power.
For his word
was like a burning fire
penetrating the innermost depths of the heart;
and it filled the minds of all
with admiration,
since it made no pretense
at the elegance of human composition
but exuded the perfume
of divine revelation.

Once when he was to preach in the presence of the pope and cardinals at the suggestion of the lord cardinal of Ostia, he memorized a sermon which he had carefully composed. When he stood in their midst to present his edifying words, he went completely blank and was unable to say anything at all. This he admitted to them in true humility and directed himself to invoke the grace of the Holy Spirit. Suddenly he began to overflow with such effective eloquence and to move the minds of those high-ranking men to compunction with such force and power that it was clearly evident it was not he but the Spirit of the Lord who *was* speaking.

Because he had first convinced himself by practice of what he persuaded others to do by his words, he did not fear reproof but preached the truth most confidently. He did not know how to touch the faults of others gingerly but only how to lance them; nor did he foster the habits of sinners but struck at them with harsh reproaches. He used to speak with the same firmness of mind to the great and the small and with the same joy of spirit to

a few or to many. People of every age and sex hastened to see and
hear this new man sent to the world by heaven.

> Traveling through various regions,
> he preached the Gospel
> with burning love,
> as the Lord worked with him and confirmed his
>   preaching
> with the signs that followed.
> For in the power of the name of God,
> Francis, the herald of truth,
> cast out devils and healed the sick,
> and what is greater,
> softened the obstinate hearts of sinners
> and moved them to repentance,
> restoring at the same time health
> to their bodies and hearts,
> as his miracles prove,
> a few of which we will cite below as examples.

In the town of Toscanella he was warmly received and given hospitality by a certain knight whose only son had been crippled
since birth. At the father's insistent pleading, Francis lifted the
child up with his hand and cured him instantly, so that all the
limbs of his body at once got back their strength in view of all;
and the boy became healthy and strong and immediately rose,
walking and leaping and praising God.

In the town of Narni, at the request of the bishop, Francis made
the sign of the cross from head to foot over a paralytic who had

lost the use of all his limbs, and restored him to perfect health.

In the diocese of Rieti a boy was so swollen for four years that he could not see his own legs. When the boy was presented to Francis by his tearful mother, he was cured the moment the holy man touched him with his sacred hands.

At the town of Orte a boy was so twisted that his head was bent down to his feet and some of his bones were broken. When Francis made the sign of the cross over him at the tearful entreaty of his parents, he was cured on the spot and stretched out immediately.

There was a woman in the town of Gubbio whose hands were so withered and crippled that she could do nothing with them. When Francis made the sign of the cross over them in the name of the Lord, she was so perfectly cured that she immediately went home and prepared with her own hands food for him and for the poor, like Peter's mother-in-law (Matt. 8:14–15).

In the village of Bevagna he marked the eyes of a blind girl with his spittle three times in the name of the Trinity and restored the sight she longed for.

A woman of the town of Narni who had been struck blind received from him the sign of the cross and recovered the sight she longed for.

At Bologna a boy had one eye covered over with an opaque film so that he could see nothing at all with it nor could he be helped by any treatment. After God's servant had made the sign of the cross from his head to his feet, he recovered his sight so completely that, having later entered the Order of Friars Minor, he claimed that he could see far more clearly with the eye that had been previously ill than with the eye that had always been well.

In the village of Sangemini God's servant was given hospitality by a devoted man whose wife was troubled by a devil. After praying, Francis commanded the devil to depart in virtue of obedience, and by God's power drove him out so suddenly that it became evident that the obstinacy of devils cannot resist the power of holy obedience.

In Città di Castello an evil spirit which had taken possession of a woman departed full of indignation when commanded under obedience by the holy man, and left the woman who had been possessed free in body and mind.

A friar was suffering from such a horrible illness that many were convinced it was more a case of possession by the devil than a natural sickness. For he was often cast down and rolled about foaming at the mouth, with his limbs now contracted, now stretched out, now folded, now twisted, now rigid and hard. Sometimes, when he was stretched out and rigid, he would be lifted into the air with his feet level with his head and then would fall down horribly. Christ's servant was full of pity for him in such a miserable and incurable illness, and he sent him a morsel of the bread he was eating. When he tasted the bread, the sick man received such strength that he never suffered from that illness again.

In the district of Arezzo a woman had been in labor for several days and was already near death; there was no cure left for her in her desperate state except from God. Christ's servant was passing

through that region, riding on horseback because of physical illness. It happened that when the animal was being returned to its
owner, it was led through the village where the woman was suffering. When the men of the place saw the horse on which the
holy man had been mounted, they took off the reins and placed
them on the woman. As soon as the reins touched her, all danger
miraculously passed, and she gave birth safely.

A man from Città della Pieve, who was religious and God-fearing, had in his possession a cord which our holy father had worn
around his waist. Since many men and women in that town were
suffering from various forms of illness, he went to the homes of
the sick and gave the patients water to drink in which he had
dipped the cord. In this way many were cured.

Sick persons who ate bread touched by the man of God were
quickly restored to health by divine power.

> Since the herald of Christ
> in his preaching
> brilliantly shone with these and many other
>   miracles,
> people paid attention to what he said
> as if an angel of the Lord were speaking.
> His extraordinary achievement in virtue,
> his spirit of prophecy,
> the power of his miracles,
> his mission to preach conferred from heaven,
> the obedience paid him by creatures lacking
>   reason,

the powerful change of heart experienced
at the hearing of his words,
his being instructed by the Holy Spirit
on a level beyond human teaching,
his authorization to preach
granted by the Supreme Pontiff
who was guided by a revelation,
the Rule, in which the manner of preaching is
    described,
confirmed by the same Vicar of Christ,
and the marks of the Supreme King
imprinted on his body like a seal—
these are like ten witnesses
which testify without any doubt to the whole
    world
that Francis, the herald of Christ,
is worthy of veneration because of his mission,
authoritative in his teaching,
admirable for his holiness,
and therefore he preached the Gospel of Christ
as a true messenger of God.

Chapter 13

On His Sacred Stigmata

The angelic man Francis
had made it his habit
never to relax in his pursuit of the good.
Rather, like the heavenly spirits on Jacob's
  ladder
he either ascended to God
or descended to his neighbor.
For he had wisely learned
so to divide the time given to him for merit
that he expended part of it in working for his
  neighbor's benefit
and devoted the other part
to the peaceful ecstasy of contemplation.
Therefore when in his compassion he had
  worked
for the salvation of others,
he would then leave behind the restlessness of
  the crowds
and seek out hidden places
of quiet and solitude,
where he could spend his time more freely
with the Lord
and cleanse himself of any dust
that might have adhered to him
from his involvement with men.

Two years
before he gave his spirit back to heaven,
after many and varied labors,
he was led apart by divine providence
to a high place
which is called Mount La Verna.
When according to his usual custom
he had begun to fast there for forty days
in honor of St. Michael the Archangel,
he experienced more abundantly than usual
an overflow of the sweetness of heavenly
   contemplation,
he burned with a stronger flame
of heavenly desires,
and he began to experience more fully
the gifts of heavenly grace.
He was borne aloft
not like one who out of curiosity
searches into the supreme majesty
only to be crushed by its glory,
but like the faithful and prudent servant
searching out God's good pleasure,
to which he desires with the greatest ardor
to conform himself in every way.

Through divine inspiration he had learned that if he opened the
book of the Gospels, Christ would reveal to him what God considered most acceptable in him and from him. After praying with
much devotion, he took the book of the Gospels from the altar
and had his companion, a holy man dedicated to God, open it

three times in the name of the Holy Trinity. When all three times the book was opened the Lord's passion always met his eyes, the man filled with God understood that just as he had imitated Christ in the actions of his life, so he should be conformed to him in the affliction and sorrow of his passion, before he would pass out of this world. And although his body was already weakened by the great austerity of his past life and his continual carrying of the Lord's cross, he was in no way terrified but was inspired even more vigorously to endure martyrdom. His unquenchable fire of love for the good Jesus had been fanned into such a blaze of flames that many waters could not quench so powerful a love.

By the Seraphic ardor of his desires, he was being borne aloft into God; and by his sweet compassion he was being transformed into him who chose to be crucified because of the excess of his love. On a certain morning about the feast of the Exaltation of the Cross, while Francis was praying on the mountainside, he saw a Seraph with six fiery and shining wings descend from the height of heaven. And when in swift flight the Seraph had reached a spot in the air near the man of God, there appeared between the wings the figure of a man crucified, with his hands and feet extended in the form of a cross and fastened to a cross. Two of the wings were lifted above his head, two were extended for flight and two covered his whole body. When Francis saw this, he was overwhelmed and his heart was flooded with a mixture of joy and sorrow. He rejoiced because of the gracious way Christ looked upon him under the appearance of the Seraph, but the fact that he was fastened to a cross pierced his soul with a sword of compassionate sorrow.

He wondered exceedingly at the sight of so unfathomable a vision, realizing that the weakness of Christ's passion was in no way compatible with the immortality of the Seraph's spiritual nature. Eventually he understood by a revelation from the Lord that divine providence had shown him this vision so that, as Christ's lover, he might learn in advance that he was to be totally transformed into the likeness of Christ crucified, not by the martyrdom of his flesh, but by the fire of his love consuming his soul.

As the vision disappeared, it left in his heart a marvelous ardor and imprinted on his body markings that were no less marvelous. Immediately the marks of nails began to appear in his hands and feet just as he had seen a little before in the figure of the man crucified. His hands and feet seemed to be pierced through the center by nails, with the heads of the nails appearing on the inner side of the hands and the upper side of the feet and their points on the opposite sides. The heads of the nails in his hands and his feet were round and black; their points were oblong and bent as if driven back with a hammer, and they emerged from the flesh and stuck out beyond it. Also his right side, as if pierced with a lance, was marked with a red wound from which his sacred blood often flowed, moistening his tunic and underwear.

When Christ's servant realized that he could not conceal from his intimate companions the stigmata that had been so visibly imprinted on his flesh, he feared to make public the Lord's secret and was thrown into an agony of doubt whether to tell what he had seen or to be silent about it. He called some of the friars and, speaking in general terms, presented his doubt to them and sought their advice. One of the friars, who was named Illuminato and was illumined by grace, realized that Francis had had a miraculous vision because he seemed still completely dazed. He said to the holy man: "Brother, you should realize that at times divine secrets are revealed to you not for yourself alone but also for others. You have every reason to fear that if you hide what you have received for the profit of many, you will be blamed for 'burying that talent'" (Matt. 25:25). Although the holy man used to say on other occasions, "My secret is for myself," he was moved by Illuminato's words and then with much fear recounted the vision in detail, adding that the one who had appeared to him had told him some things which he would never disclose to any man as long as he lived. We should believe, then, that those things he had been told by that sacred Seraph who had miraculously appeared to him on the cross were so secret that "men are not permitted to speak of them" (2 Cor. 12:4).

> When the true love of Christ
> had transformed his lover into his image
> and the forty days were over
> that he had planned to spend in solitude,
> and the feast of St. Michael the Archangel
> had also arrived,
> the angelic man Francis
> came down from the mountain,

bearing with him
the image of the Crucified,
which was depicted not on tablets of stone
or on panels of wood
by the hands of a craftsman,
but engraved in the members of his body
by the finger of the living God.
Because it is good to keep hidden
the secret of the King,
Francis,
aware that he had been given a royal secret,
to the best of his powers
kept the sacred stigmata hidden.
Since it is for God to reveal for his own glory
the wonders which he has performed,
the Lord himself,
who had secretly imprinted those marks on
    Francis,
publicly worked through them
a number of miracles
so that the miraculous though hidden
power of the stigmata
might be made manifest
by the brightness of divine signs.

In the province of Rieti a very serious plague broke out and so cruelly took the lives of cattle and sheep that no remedy could be found. A certain God-fearing man was told in a vision at night to hurry to the hermitage of the friars and get the water in which God's servant Francis, who was staying there at that time, had washed his hands and feet and to sprinkle it on all the animals. He got up in the morning, came to the hermitage, secretly got the water from the companions of the holy man and sprinkled it on the sheep and cattle. Marvelous to say, the moment that water touched the animals, which were weak and lying on the ground, they immediately recovered their former vigor, stood up and, as if they had had nothing wrong with them, hurried off to pasture. Thus through the miraculous power of that water, which had touched his sacred wounds, the plague ceased and deadly disease fled from the flocks.

Before the holy man stayed on Mount La Verna, clouds would often form over the mountain, and violent hailstorms would devastate the crops. But after his blessed vision the hail stopped permanently, to the amazement of the inhabitants, so that the unusually serene face of the sky proclaimed the extraordinary nature of his heavenly vision and the power of the stigmata that were imprinted on him there.

In wintertime because of his physical weakness and the rough roads Francis was once riding on a donkey belonging to a poor man. It happened that he spent the night at the base of an overhanging cliff to try to avoid the inconveniences of a snowfall and the darkness of night that prevented him from reaching his place of lodging. The saint heard his helper tossing and turning, grumbling and groaning, since, as he had only thin clothing, the biting cold would not let him sleep. Francis, burning with the fire of divine love, stretched out his hand and touched him. A marvelous thing happened! At the touch of his sacred hand, which bore the burning coal of the Seraph, immediately the cold fled altogether, and the man felt great heat within and without, as if he had been hit by a fiery blast from the vent of a furnace. Comforted in mind and body, he slept until morning more soundly among the rocks and snow than he ever had in his own bed, as he used to say later.

> Thus it is established by convincing evidence
> that these sacred marks were imprinted on him
> by the power of the One
> who purifies, illumines and inflames
> through the action of the Seraphim.
> With their miraculous power
> these sacred marks,
> in the external realm,
> restored health by purifying from a pestilence,
> produced serene skies,
> and gave heat to the body.
> After his death
> this was demonstrated
> by even more evident miracles
> as we will record in the proper place later.

Although he tried his best to hide the "treasure found in the field" (Matt. 13:44), he could not prevent at least some from seeing the stigmata in his hands and feet, although he always kept his hands covered and from that time on always wore shoes. A number of the friars saw them while he was still alive. Although they were men of outstanding holiness and so completely trustworthy, nevertheless to remove all doubt they confirmed under oath, touching the holy Gospels, that this was so and that they had seen it. Also some of the cardinals saw them because of their close friendship with the holy man; and they inserted praises of the sacred stigmata in the hymns, antiphons and sequences which they composed in his honor, and thus by their words and writings gave testimony to the truth. Even the Supreme Pontiff Lord Alexander, in a sermon preached to the people at which many of the friars and I myself were present, affirmed that he had seen the sacred stigmata with his own eyes while the saint was still alive. More than fifty friars with the virgin Clare, who was most devoted to God, and her sisters, as well as innumerable laymen saw them after his death. Many of them kissed the stigmata out of devotion and touched them with their own hands to strengthen their testimony, as we will describe in the proper place.

But the wound in his side he so cautiously concealed that as long as he was alive no one could see it except by stealth. One friar who used to zealously take care of him induced him with a pious strategem to take off his tunic to shake it out. Watching closely, he saw the wound, and he even quickly touched it with three of his fingers, determining the size of the wound by both sight and touch. The friar who was his vicar at that time also managed to see it by a similar strategem. A friar who was a companion of his, a man of marvelous simplicity, when he was one day massaging Francis's shoulders that were weak from illness, put his hand under his hood and accidentally touched the sacred wound, causing him great pain. As a result, from that time on Francis always wore underclothes made so that they would reach up to his armpits to cover the wound on his side. Also the friars who washed these or shook out his tunic from time to time,

since they found these stained with blood, were from this evident
sign convinced without any doubt of the existence of the sacred
wound, which after his death they along with many others con-
templated and venerated with unveiled face.

> Come now, knight of Christ,
> vigorously bear the arms of your
>   unconquerable Leader!
> Visibly shielded with these,
> you will overcome all adversaries.
> Carry the standard of the Most High King,
> and at its sight
> let all who fight in God's army
> be aroused to courage.
> Carry the seal of Christ, the High Priest,
> by which your words and deeds
> will be rightly accepted by all
> as authentic and beyond reproach.
> For now because of the brand-marks of the
>   Lord Jesus
> which you carry in your body,
> no one should trouble you;
> rather every servant of Christ
> should show them deep devotion.
> Now through these most certain signs
> (corroborated
> not by the sufficient testimony
> of two or three witnesses,
> but by the superabundant testimony
> of a whole multitude)

God's testimony about you and through you
has been made overwhelmingly credible,
removing completely from unbelievers
the veil of excuse,
while these signs confirm believers in faith,
raise them aloft with confident hope
and set them ablaze with the fire of charity.

Now is fulfilled
the first vision which you saw,
namely, that you would be a captain
in the army of Christ
and bear the arms of heaven
emblazoned with the sign of the cross.
Now is fulfilled
the vision of the Crucified
at the beginning of your conversion
which pierced your soul
with a sword of compassionate sorrow.
Now the voice that came from the cross
as if from the lofty throne and secret mercy-seat
    of Christ,
as you have confirmed with your sacred words,
is believed as undoubtedly true.
Now is fulfilled
the vision of the cross,
in the course of your conversion,
which Brother Silvester saw
marvelously coming from your mouth;
and the vision which the holy Pacificus saw,
of the swords piercing your body

in the form of a cross;
and the sight of you
lifted up in the air in the form of a cross,
which the angelic man Monaldus saw
when the holy Anthony was preaching
on the inscription on the cross—
all of these
we now firmly believe
were not imaginary visions
but revelations from heaven.
Now, finally
toward the end of your life
you were shown at the same time
the sublime vision of the Seraph
and the humble figure of the Crucified,
inwardly inflaming you and outwardly
    marking you
as the second Angel,
ascending from the rising of the sun
and bearing upon you the sign of the
    living God.
This vision confirms the previous ones
and receives from them
the testimony of truth.
Behold
these seven visions of the cross of Christ,
miraculously shown and manifested
to you or about you
at different stages of your life.
The first six were like steps
leading to the seventh

in which you have found your final rest.
The cross of Christ
given to you and by you accepted
at the beginning of your conversion
and which from then on
you carried continuously
in the course of your most upright life,
giving an example to others,
shows that you have finally reached
the summit of Gospel perfection
with such clear certitude
that no truly devout person
can reject this proof of Christian wisdom
plowed into the dust of your flesh.
No truly believing person can attack it,
no truly humble person can make little of it,
since it is truly the work of God
and worthy of complete acceptance.

Chapter 14

On His Patience and His Passing in Death

> Now fixed with Christ to the cross,
> in both body and spirit,
> Francis
> not only burned with a Seraphic love of God
> but also thirsted with Christ crucified
> for the salvation of men.

Since he could not walk because of the nails protruding from his feet, he had his half-dead body carried through the towns and villages to arouse others to carry the cross of Christ. He used to say to the friars: "Let us begin, brothers, to serve the Lord our God, for up to now we have hardly progressed." He was ablaze with a great desire to return to the humility he practiced at the beginning; to nurse the lepers as he did at the outset and to treat like a slave once more his body that was already in a state of collapse from his work. With Christ as his leader, he proposed to do great things; and although his limbs were failing, he bravely and fervently hoped to conquer the enemy in a new combat. Laziness and idleness have no place where the goad of love never ceases to drive a person to greater things. His body was so much in harmony with his spirit and so ready to obey it that when he strove to attain complete holiness, his body not only did not resist, but even tried to run ahead.

In order that his merits might increase—for these are brought to perfection in patient suffering—the man of God began to suffer from various illnesses, so seriously that scarcely any part of his body remained free from intense pain and suffering. Through varied, prolonged and continual illness he was brought to the point where his flesh was already wasted away, as if nothing but skin clung to his bones. But when he was tortured by harsh bodily suffering, he called his trials not by the name of torments but sisters.

Once when he was suffering more intensely than usual, a certain friar in his simplicity told him: "Brother, pray to the Lord that he treat you more mildly, for he seems to have laid his hand on you more heavily than he should." At these words, the holy man wailed and cried out: "If I did not know your simplicity and sincerity, then I would from now on shrink from your company because you dared to call into judgment God's judgments upon me." Even though he was completely worn out by his prolonged and serious illness, he threw himself on the ground, bruising his weakened bones in the hard fall. Kissing the ground, he said: "I thank you, Lord God, for all these sufferings; and I ask you, my Lord, to increase them a hundredfold if it pleases you, for it will be most acceptable to me. 'Afflict me with suffering and do not spare me' (Job 6:10), since to do your will is an overflowing consolation for me." So it seemed to the friars as if they were seeing another Job, whose vigor of soul increased with the increase of his bodily weariness. He knew long in advance the time of his death, and as the day of his passing grew near, he told the friars that he should soon lay aside the tent of his body, as it had been revealed to him by Christ.

For two years after the imprinting of the sacred stigmata—that is, in the twentieth year of his conversion—under the many blows of agonizing illness he was squared like a stone to be fitted into the construction of the heavenly Jerusalem and like a work of wrought metal he was brought to perfection by the hammer of many tribulations. Then he asked to be carried to St. Mary of the Portiuncula so that he might yield up the spirit of life where he had received the spirit of grace. When he had been brought there, in that last illness that was being concluded in a state of complete weakness, he wished to show by the example of Truth itself that he had nothing in common with the world. And so, in fervor of spirit, he threw himself totally naked on the naked ground so that in that final hour of death, when the enemy could still attack him violently, he would struggle naked with a naked enemy. Lying like this on the ground stripped of his garments of sackcloth, he lifted his face to heaven in his accustomed way and gave his whole attention to its glory, covering the wound in his right side with his left hand lest it be seen. And he said to his friars: "I have done my duty; may Christ teach you yours."

Pierced with the spear of compassion, the companions of the saint wept bitterly. The one among them whom the man of God used to call his guardian, knowing his wish through divine inspiration, hurriedly arose, took a tunic along with a cord and underclothes, and offered them to the little poor man of Christ, saying: "I am lending these to you as to a beggar, and you are to accept them under the command of obedience." The holy man was happy at this and rejoiced in the gladness of his heart because he saw that he had been faithful to his Lady Poverty up to the end. Raising his hands to heaven, he glorified his Christ because he was going to him, free and unburdened by anything. He had done all this out of his zeal for poverty, for he did not even want to have a habit unless it were lent to him by another.

> In all things
> he wished to be conformed to Christ crucified,
> who hung on the cross
> poor, suffering and naked.
> Therefore at the beginning of his conversion,
> he stood naked before the bishop,
> and at the end of his life,
> naked he wished to go out of this world.
> He enjoined the friars assisting him,
> under obedience and charity,
> that when they saw he was dead,
> they should allow
> his body to lie naked on the ground
> for the length of time
> it takes to walk a leisurely mile.
> O, he was truly the most Christian of men,
> for he strove to conform himself to Christ
> and to imitate him perfectly—
> while living to imitate Christ living,
> dying to imitate Christ dying,
> and after death to imitate Christ after death—
> and he merited to be honored
> with the imprint of Christ's likeness!

When the hour of his passing was approaching, he had all the friars who were there called to him and, consoling them for his death with words of comfort, he exhorted them with fatherly affection to love God. He long continued speaking about practicing poverty and patience and about keeping the faith of the Holy Roman Church, and he recommended the Gospel to them before any other rule of life. While all the friars were sitting around him, he extended his hands over them, crossing his arms in the form of a cross—for he always loved this sign—and he blessed all the friars, both present and absent, in the name and power of Christ crucified. Then he added: "Farewell, all my sons, in the fear of the Lord; remain in it always! Temptation and tribulation are coming in the near future, but happy are they who will persevere in what they have begun. I am hastening to God, to whose grace I commend you all." When he finished this gentle admonition, the man beloved of God ordered the book of the Gospels to be brought to him and asked that the Gospel according to John be read to him from the place that begins: "Before the feast of Passover" (John 13:1). He himself, insofar as he was able, broke out with this psalm: "I have cried to the Lord with my voice, with my voice I have implored the Lord" (Ps. 141:2); and he finished it to the end: "The just will await me until you have rewarded me" (Ps. 141:2, 141:7).

At last, when all of God's mysteries were fulfilled in him and his most holy soul was freed from his body to be absorbed in the abyss of the divine light, the blessed man fell asleep in the Lord. One of his brothers and disciples saw his blessed soul under the appearance of a radiant star being carried aloft on a shining cloud over many waters on a direct path into heaven. It shone with the brightness of sublime sanctity and was full of the abundance of heavenly wisdom and grace by which the holy man had merited to enter the place of light and peace where forever he rests with Christ.

At that time the minister of the friars in Terra di Lavoro was Brother Augustine, a holy and upright man, who was near death and had already for a long time lost his power of speech. Suddenly he cried out in the hearing of those who were standing about: "Wait for me, Father, wait for me. Wait, I am coming with you!" Amazed, the friars asked to whom he was speaking so boldly. He replied: "Don't you see our father Francis on his way to heaven?" And at once his holy soul left his body and followed his most holy father.

The bishop of Assisi was gone at that time on a pilgrimage to the shrine of St. Michael on Monte Gargano. Blessed Francis appeared to him on the night of his passing and said: "Behold, I leave the world and go to heaven." Rising in the morning, the bishop told his companions what he had seen, and returning to Assisi, he carefully inquired and found out with certainty that the blessed father had departed this world at the very hour when he appeared to him in this vision.

> Larks are birds
> that love the light and dread the twilight
>   darkness.

But at the hour of the holy man's passing,
although it was twilight and night was to
    follow,
they came in a great flock
over the roof of the house
and, whirling around for a long time
with unusual joy,
gave clear and evident testimony
of the glory of the saint,
who so often had invited them
to praise God.

Chapter 15

On His Canonization and the Solemn Transferal of His Body

Francis,
the servant and friend of the Most High,
the founder and leader of the Order of Friars
    Minor,
the practitioner of poverty, the model of
    penance,
the herald of truth, the mirror of holiness
and the exemplar of all Gospel perfection,
foreordained by grace from heaven,
in an ordered progression
from the lowest level reached the very heights.
This remarkable man—
rich in poverty, exalted in humility,
full of life in the midst of mortification,
wise in simplicity,
outstanding for the excellence of the total
    conduct of his life—
this remarkable man God made remarkably
    renowned
in his life
and incomparably more renowned
in his death.
When this blessed man

traveled away from this world,
his sacred spirit,
as it entered his home of eternity,
was glorified by a full draft from the fountain
   of life
and left certain signs of future glory
imprinted on his body,
so that his most holy flesh,
which had been crucified along with its
   passions
and transformed into a new creature,
might bear the image of Christ's passion
by a singular privilege
and prefigure the resurrection
by this unprecedented miracle.

In his blessed hands and feet could be seen the nails that had been miraculously formed out of his flesh by divine power. They were so embedded in the flesh that when they were pressed on one side, they immediately stuck out the other, as if they were continuous hardened sinews. Also the wound in his side could be clearly seen, which was not inflicted on his body nor produced by human means; it was like the wound in the Savior's side, which brought forth in our Redeemer the mystery of the redemption and regeneration of the human race. The nails were black like iron; the wound in his side was red, and because it was drawn into a kind of circle by the contraction of the flesh looked like a most beautiful rose. The rest of his skin, which before was inclined to be dark both naturally and from his illness, now shone with a dazzling whiteness, prefiguring the beauty of that glorious second stole.

His limbs were so supple and soft to the touch that they seemed to have regained the tenderness of childhood and to be adorned with clear signs of his innocence. The nails appeared black against his shining skin, and the wound in his side was red like a rose in springtime so that it is no wonder the onlookers were amazed and overjoyed at the sight of such varied and miraculous beauty. His sons were weeping at the loss of so lovable a father but were filled with no little joy when they kissed on his body the seal-marks of the supreme King. This unprecedented miracle turned their grief into joy and transported into amazement their attempts at comprehending it. So unique and so remarkable was the sight to all who observed it that it confirmed their faith and incited their love. It was a matter of amazement to those who heard of it, and aroused their desire to see it.

When the people heard of the passing of our blessed father and news of the miracle had spread, they hurried to the place to see with their own eyes so that they could dispel all doubt and add joy to their love. A great number of the citizens of Assisi were admitted to see the sacred stigmata with their own eyes and to kiss them with their lips. One of them, a knight who was educated and prudent, Jerome by name, a distinguished and famous man, had doubts about these sacred signs and was unbelieving like Thomas. Fervently and boldly, in the presence of the friars and the citizens, he did not hesitate to move the nails and to touch with his hands the saint's hands, feet and side. While he was examining with his hands these authentic signs of Christ's wounds, he completely healed the wound of doubt in his own heart and the hearts of others. As a result, later along with others he became a firm witness to this truth which he had come to know with such certainty; and he swore to it on the Gospel.

His brothers and sons, who had been summoned to their father's passing, along with a great number of people spent that night in which the blessed confessor of Christ departed singing the divine praises in such a way that it seemed to be a vigil of angels and not a wake for the dead. In the morning, the crowds that had assembled took branches from the trees and with a blaze of many candles carried his sacred body to the town of Assisi, singing hymns and canticles. As they passed the church of San Damiano, where the noble virgin Clare, who is now glorious in heaven, lived at that time cloistered with her nuns, they stopped there for a short while so that those holy nuns could see and kiss his sacred body, adorned with its heavenly pearls. When they arrived at the city with great rejoicing, they reverently placed in the church of St. George the precious treasure they were carrying. It was there that he had gone to school as a little boy and there that he first preached and there, finally, that he found his first place of rest.

Our venerable father left the shipwreck of this world in the year of the Lord's Incarnation 1226, on Saturday evening, October 3, and was buried on Sunday.

> Immediately
> the holy man began
> to reflect the light radiating from the face of God
> and to sparkle

with many great miracles
so that the sublimity of his holiness,
which, while he was still in the flesh,
had been known to the world as a guide for
    conduct
through examples of perfect righteousness,
now that he is reigning with Christ
was approved from heaven
as a confirmation of faith
through miracles performed by the divine
    power.
In different parts of the world,
his glorious miracles
and the abundant blessings obtained
    through him
inflamed many to devotion to Christ
and incited them to reverence for his saint.
The wonderful things
which God was working
through his servant Francis—
acclaimed by word of mouth
and testified to by facts—
came to the ears
of the Supreme Pontiff, Gregory IX.

That shepherd of the Church was fully convinced of Francis's
remarkable holiness, not only from the miracles he heard of after
the saint's death, but also from his own experience during his
life, having seen with his own eyes and touched with his own
hands; consequently he had no doubt that Francis was glorified

in heaven by the Lord. In order to act in conformity with Christ, whose vicar he was, after prayerful consideration he decided to glorify him on earth by proclaiming him worthy of all veneration. In order to certify to the whole world the glorification of this most holy man, he had the known miracles recorded and attested to by appropriate witness. These he submitted to the examination of those cardinals who seemed less favorable to his cause. This material was examined carefully and approved by all. With the unanimous advice and assent of his confreres and of all the prelates who were then in the curia, he decreed that Francis should be canonized. He came personally to Assisi in the year of the Lord's Incarnation 1228 on Sunday, July 16, and inscribed our blessed father in the catalog of the saints, in a great and solemn ceremony that would be too long to describe.

In the year of Our Lord 1230, when the friars had assembled for a general chapter at Assisi, Francis's body, which had been so dedicated to God, was solemnly transferred on May 25 to the basilica constructed in his honor.

> While that sacred treasure was being carried,
> marked with the seal of the Most High King,
> he whose image Francis bore
> deigned to perform many miracles
> so that through his saving fragrance
> the faithful in their love
> might be drawn to run after Christ.
> It was truly appropriate
> that he who was pleasing to God and beloved
>   by him

in his life;
who, like Enoch,
had been borne into paradise
by the grace of contemplation
and carried off to heaven
like Elijah in a fiery chariot;
now that his soul is blossoming
in eternal springtime
among the heavenly flowers
it was, indeed, truly appropriate
that his blessed bones too
should sprout with fragrant miracles
in their own place of rest.
Just as that blessed man
shone in his life
with the marvelous signs of virtue,
so from the day of his passing to the present,
in different parts of the world,
he radiated forth
with outstanding miracles
through the divine power that glorified him.
For the blind and the deaf,
the mute and the crippled,
paralytics and those suffering from dropsy,
lepers and those possessed by devils,
the shipwrecked and the captives—
all these were given relief
through his merits.
For every disease, every need, every danger,
he offered a remedy.
Many dead, even,

were miraculously brought back to life
through him.
Thus the magnificence
of the power of the Most High
doing wonders for his saint
shines forth to the faithful.
To him be honor and glory
for endless ages of ages.
Amen.

Here Ends the Life of Blessed Francis